TIME

WHAT IS OCCUPY?

Inside the Global Movement

1

Published by TIME Books,
an imprint of Time Home Entertainment Inc.
135 West 50th Street, New York, NY 10020

ISBN 10: 1-60320-941-7
ISBN 13: 978-1-60320-941-0

We welcome your comments and suggestions about TIME Books.
Please write to us at:
TIME Books, Attention: Book Editors,
P.O. Box 11016, Des Moines, IA
50336-1016

If you would like to order any of our hardcover Collector's Edition
books, please call us at 1-800-327-6388 , Monday through Friday,
7 a.m. to 8 p.m., or Saturday, 7 a.m. to 6 p.m., Central Time.

BACK COVER: Timothy A. Clary/AFP/Getty Images

CONTENTS

Foreword

What is "Occupy Wall Street"? When that search term on Google surpassed "Tea Party" in popularity (on Sept. 24, 2011), a new movement had arrived, signified by the online curiosity about its followers, its beliefs and its impact. At TIME and TIME.com, we've closely followed its rise, not just the daily happenings at the encampments at Manhattan's Zuccotti Park, in Oakland, Calif., and many other cities, but also the social conditions that gave rise to the movement. In our stories about the decline of social mobility in the U.S., the new generation gap and the 22-year-old who took on Bank of America over its fees, TIME has tapped into the reasons for rising anger of the so-called 99% and economic justice as incendiary new topics in the public arena. In this new book, which went to press on the two-month anniversary of the movement's founding, we bring you these stories from the magazine and the website, plus new stories on the political effects of the movement, the key moments of its early days and its global resonance. We also present a forum of prominent voices, both supportive and critical of the movement. Besides covering the story, TIME is a co-convener of Opportunity Nation, a broad-based nonpartisan coalition of more than 125 organizations trying to increase social mobility in America. It's an issue whose time has come.

From the Editors of TIME
Nov. 17, 2011

Introduction:
Taking It to the Streets
BY MICHAEL SCHERER

On its two-month anniversary, something shifted for Occupy Wall Street. The remaining encampments were vacated, and thousands marched through America's largest cities. They shut down intersections in Los Angeles and entered banks in Portland, Ore. They swarmed bridges in Washington, Seattle and Manhattan and filled city streets in Chicago. Arrests were commonplace, and the tension was palpable. But beneath the din and shoving matches with police, the nascent movement that had changed American politics was sending a clear message. Though the permanent tent encampments were dwindling in the face of winter and rising lawlessness, the movement would not end. There would be a new phase, and it would be everywhere.

On this point, few in power disagreed. "We're coming to a point where Occupy Wall Street is just the beginning," warned New York City mayor Michael Bloomberg that very morning, on Nov. 17, in a midtown address to business leaders, taking note of growing economic fears. "The public is getting scared. They don't know what to do, and they're going to strike out, and they don't know where." In the fall of 2011, Occupy provided that outlet—for the economic anxiety, the collective sense of injustice and the rising feeling of hopelessness. The protesters had filled a hole in the American experience in the most unexpected way.

It had started in Canada, of all places, with the editors of the Vancouver-based, anticonsumerist magazine *Adbusters*. They called for a Tahrir Square "moment" on Sept. 17, in lower Manhattan, a protest against "corporate rule" announced in a tweet that ended #occupywallstreet. The first responders were a motley collection of punks, anarchists, socialists, hackers, liberals and artists. They organized themselves beneath the skyscrapers of American finance, in an acre-sized plaza called Zuccotti Park nearly equidistant from Ground Zero, the New York Stock Exchange and the New York Federal Reserve. They spent the night. Then they did it again.

Others noticed: the unemployed and the underemployed, scenesters and community organizers, young people burdened by student loans, middle-aged activists and folks who never bothered to vote. The crowds swelled, both in the park and online. Camera crews arrived, prompting the curiosity of White House and congressional leaders. Suddenly there were hundreds every day. Celebrities made pilgrimages—Jay-Z, Michael Moore, Alec Baldwin and Cornel West. The spark had started a fire.

Facebook sign-up data suggest the Occupy Wall Street movement doubled in size, on average, every three days through its first month. By October, protesters in almost every state had joined in, and demonstrations had jumped both oceans to Hong Kong, Madrid, Tokyo, Frankfurt and Sydney. Occupy was now in hundreds of cities. Crowds gathered in Los Angeles, Albuquerque, Toledo, Knoxville and Fairbanks. Some rallies brought out only a few dozen, some thousands.

The growing numbers raised urgent questions: What do they want? Who are they? Where will they take this? The answers were as varied as the faces in the park. Some spoke of achieving "collective liberation," others of imposing new taxes on financial transactions. Some came to declare their desperation, others to model a new way of life. Like the student radicals who laid siege inside the Sorbonne in 1968, these newcomers organized themselves around a radical democratic campfire called the "general assembly." Barred from using bullhorns, they echoed one another's words to amplify them, and adopted hand signals to show their opposition or support.

Over time, themes emerged. Slogans came into being. The protesters claimed to represent the vast majority of the country, "the 99%," which has been languishing economically for years while the wealthiest flourish. Corporations, they said, have too much influence in Washington. Wall Street leaders, they argued, still faced a reckoning for the failings that brought on the financial crisis.

Suddenly the power structure had to respond. Federal Reserve Chairman Ben Bernanke and Treasury Secretary Tim Geithner said they understood the frustration. House Republican leader Eric Cantor warned of "growing mobs," then backtracked and acknowledged the mobs' concerns. Those with the most power, it turned out, had the best understanding of the influence of the streets. In this new decade of economic and political peril, of discredited institutions and shrinking leadership, the street protesters set the agenda. Spontaneous activism, organized through social media, had toppled Arab dictatorships and rattled advanced democracies.

It had already happened once before in the U.S. In 2009 a few dozen conservative activists found one another on Twitter and decided to call themselves the Tea Party. That group came to define the political conversation in the U.S., helping deliver Republican control of Congress in 2010. Now the left, with tents and sleeping bags, was fighting back with a similar toolkit and its own visual iconography— fewer tricorn hats, more tattoos. Instead of liberty, the new protesters demanded opportunity and equality. Instead of federal debt, they spoke of personal debt. Instead of blam-

Occupied Territory. A TIME poll shows more voters support the protesters than the Tea Party

Are things in this country generally going in the **right direction,** or have they **pretty seriously gotten onto the wrong track?**

⟵─────────────────────────⟶

Wrong track **81%**   Right direction **14%**

PROTESTS

How do you view the **protests on Wall Street and across the nation** against policies demonstrators say favor the rich, the government's bank bailout and the influence of money in our political system?

54% Favorably

23% Unfavorably

23% Don't know enough to say

UNEMPLOYMENT BENEFITS

Do unemployment benefits **discourage people from seeking work,** or are most unemployed people **seriously looking for jobs?**

37% Unemployment benefits discourage work

52% People are seriously looking for jobs

SPENDING AND TAXES

73% of people favor **raising taxes on those with annual incomes of $1 million or more** to help cut the federal deficit

---

Is it more important for the government to **cut government spending** or to **spend more money** to stimulate the economy and create jobs?

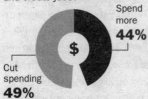

Spend more **44%**

Cut spending **49%**

What is the best way to **reduce the federal budget deficit?**

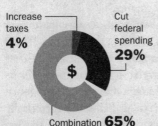

Increase taxes **4%**

Cut federal spending **29%**

Combination **65%**

TEA PARTY

What is your opinion of the **Tea Party movement?**

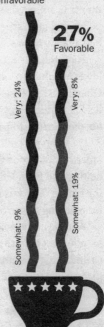

39% Don't know enough to say

33% Unfavorable

27% Favorable

Very: 24%

Very: 8%

Somewhat: 9%

Somewhat: 19%

This TIME/Abt SRBI poll was conducted by telephone Oct. 9-10 among a national random sample of 1,001 Americans ages 18 and older. The margin of error for the entire sample is ±3 percentage points. The full questionnaire and trend data may be found at www.srbi.com

ing the government, they blamed the rich.

The larger public was taking notice as well. By early October, more than half of those polled said they had heard of Occupy Wall Street, and they seemed to like it. A TIME/Abt SRBI poll found that 54% of Americans had a favorable view of the new protest movement, despite the images of bearded youth playing bongo drums and painting their bodies in Zuccotti Park. The same poll found that just 27% had a favorable view of the Tea Party. Over time, the poll numbers softened as headlines noted violent clashes with police and lawlessness amid the tents. But the new agenda had already been set.

For embattled Democrats, the American autumn in lower Manhattan looked like a revelation. President Barack Obama had struggled to get the country's attention during his September pivot to a class-based counteroffensive: a call for the wealthy to pay their "fair share" in taxes to fund a $447 billion jobs bill. Senate Democrats, for their part, embraced a 5.6% tax on those with incomes over $1 million. But neither the President's plan nor the Senate efforts stirred the nation. This was a time not for leading from the top but for listening to the bottom. Democrats wondered if the reawakening of the political left had any staying power and, if so, how best to harness it. "It has enormous potential," said Celinda Lake, a Democratic strategist. "It's the kind of thing that you want to ride but not capture."

Two years earlier, Republican political consultants were offering remarkably similar advice to their clients. "There will be no leaders to the Tea Party," the pollster Ed Goeas predicted presciently in early 2010. "What there will be is a consensus, and a belief and a direction, that is much deeper." He told Republicans to tie themselves rhetorically to the anti-incumbent, antigovernment thrust of the Tea

Party message without taking any ownership. Electoral victory would follow.

Now the conversation was shifting again. Just weeks after the first Occupation, talk of debt and deficit gave way to talk of economic justice. "Politically it looks like we are heading into a very different reality," said Justin Ruben, executive director of MoveOn.org, which has been supporting the Occupy effort. "Inequality is suddenly a topic of conversation." Seeing the potential, a coalition formed in support: labor, environmental, antiwar and minority-rights groups. The White House also took notice.

In early October, hundreds from Occupy D.C. marched past the White House to an even bigger symbol of their frustrations, the U.S. Chamber of Commerce—a limestone temple of American prosperity resplendent with Corinthian columns and carved wooden doors. "Where are the jobs?" the crowd chanted, repurposing a phrase that Republicans once used against Obama. Labor and progressive leaders, called together that same day in the Eisenhower Executive Office Building for a legislative-strategy session, quickly turned their conversation to the protesters outside. "We should all recognize that we are in a new moment," said Chuck Loveless, legislative director of AFSCME, the public employees' union, to those gathered.

The White House went out of its way to praise the protesters and present them as mainstream. "What I think is that the American people understand that not everybody's been following the rules," Obama explained in a press conference on the day protesters marched by the White House chanting, "We got sold out." Vice President Joe Biden and House minority leader Nancy Pelosi offered words of sympathy. "The protests you're seeing are the same conversations people are having in living rooms and kitchens all across America," said David Plouffe, the President's top strategist. Obama's re-election campaign called for Republicans to quickly confirm the new head of the Consumer Financial Protection Bureau and accused the GOP of being "on the side of Wall Street."

But the movement Democrats wanted to ride was also still in the process of learning to walk. Already, there were stumbles. Troublemakers, drug users and the mentally ill joined the crowds. In Oakland, some threw objects at the police, who overreacted with nonlethal rounds and tear gas; suddenly, the center of an American city looked like a riot zone. At other times, the police clearly started the trouble.

The Republican National Committee, seeing an opportunity, edited the scenes of chaos from Oakland into an advertisement as evidence of the unrest President Obama's policies have sown. "We need jobs, not intellectual theories and radical protests," said another spot, paid for by an independent conservative group, attacking Democratic Senate candidate Elizabeth Warren in Massachusetts, who had voiced support for the protesters.

Indeed, as the movement continued to grow, it was hard to divine just how it would influence the 2012 election. While the Tea Party drew people from the base of the Republican Party, most of them regular voters, this movement was filled with young people who have little history in electoral politics, much less policymaking. With winter approaching and mayors ordering tent clearings, the staying power of the new encampments was by no means guaranteed. But something had already been accomplished. A tweet had begotten an international movement. The country and the world had taken notice. Regular people, without title or appointment, had shown up to claim their own power in the public square. Something had begun.

1.

First Days of a Revolution

*How a small gathering on Wall Street stepped up,
march by march, to a history-making movement.
A TIME reporter's account*

BY NATE RAWLINGS

Occupy is, at its heart, a military term. Some force, usually
an army, seizes a piece of territory and holds it, against the
efforts of others to take it back.

On Saturday, Sept. 17, 2011, about 2,000 people assembled near the *Charging Bull* sculpture at the southern tip of
Manhattan and marched north with the intention of camp-
ing out on Wall Street. They were an eclectic group, mostly
young, typically dressed in shorts and sneakers; a few even
wore suits for the occasion. Nearly everyone was fired up
with indignation about what they saw as a culture of out-
of-control greed. At first they didn't succeed, at least geographically. Police steered them away from Wall Street, so
they made their way instead to Zuccotti Park, just around

the corner from Ground Zero.

When I wandered around Zuccotti Park that day, I counted backpacks and sleeping bags, trying to differentiate the tourists and casual marchers from those who were in it for the long haul. I came up with a couple hundred people. They would become the stalwart nucleus of the movement. Each night, several hundred and sometimes a thousand people would pack the park for the "general assembly," an open meeting in which all the protesters were allowed to speak and where they voted on major decisions. In the first 10 days, the protesters set up a kitchen, an aid station, a welcome table and a library. The base camp had been established.

The Pepper Spray Seen Round the World

One week after the Occupation began, the group organized a march two miles uptown, to Union Square. The group became disjointed and the police didn't seem prepared to handle the chaos. Cops unfurled orange nets in an effort to herd a group of protesters onto the sidewalk. Then suddenly a police officer approached a group of young women corralled behind the orange netting and fired pepper spray in a broad sweeping arc. Kalee Dedrick, 24, an activist from Albany, fell to her knees screaming in pain. Chelsea Elliott, 25, a digital imager from Brooklyn, struggled to stand. "It was incredibly painful," she told the *Village Voice*. "It feels like pouring a bottle of Tabasco all over your eyes and face. I was on the ground sobbing." The episode was caught on video and made it to YouTube within hours. Millions watched the clip, and it became a galvanizing force, drawing more and more people to check out the park. They came for the night meetings and donated their time. If they wanted to support the movement and couldn't go themselves, they could order an "Occupie" from a pizza joint across the street, to be delivered to the protesters.

At a general assembly, hip-hop mogul Russell Simmons, one of many pop-culture celebrities to visit the park, spoke to the crowd. Simmons declared he was proud of what they stood for and wanted to support them. After his speech, Simmons explained to reporters what provoked and inspired him. "You're not a socialist because you want to give people health care or a decent education," Simmons said, declaring his hope to bring thousands of people to join the movement. "These kids are so clear, so bright, so insightful," he said. "It would be very easy to bring people together."

Mass Arrest on the Brooklyn Bridge

The following Saturday, Oct. 2, organizers planned a march past City Hall and across the Brooklyn Bridge. Just before 3 p.m., leaders gathered on the park's steps near Broadway and handed out flyers explaining what to do if someone was arrested. Minutes before the march was supposed to step off, Harlem Congressman Charles Rangel arrived to address the crowd, but the old-school politician, who had been censured by Congress for ethics violations the previous year, was not the kind of leader the group wanted to hear. He barely got out a couple of sentences before he was booed off the stage and beat a hasty retreat to a waiting car.

From inside the throng, the march through lower Manhattan felt like chaos. The crush of people, more than 2,500, flowed north from their camp in Zuccotti Park toward the Brooklyn Bridge, chanting slogans that ebbed and flowed through the crowd. Drums echoed off the tall buildings that form a deep canyon along narrow streets. But from the outside, the group put on a purposeful face as it moved smoothly behind a wide banner that read, OCCUPY EVERYTHING. Demonstrator Christine Velez held a sign that poked fun at two GOP presidential candidates: I WON'T BELIEVE A CORPORATION IS A PERSON UNTIL TEXAS HANGS ONE.

Dozens of police officers on motorcycles formed a long line that kept the protesters on the sidewalk and out of the traffic, a sign that the NYPD had learned from the previous week's march to Union Square. The Occupiers' plan, on this rainy day, was to march across the mile-long Brooklyn Bridge. Protest organizers had instructed everyone at the outset not to start conflict with police or pedestrians. When the march reached the bridge, a first group made its way to the upper pedestrian walkway. There was a break in the ranks, however, and a second group, of 500 to 1,000 people, began to walk onto the Brooklyn-bound roadway, where they were sure to snarl traffic. Police later said that an officer yelled into a bullhorn for the protesters to turn around. The crowd, apparently oblivious, erupted into cheers when they hit the roadway, chanting, "Who owns this bridge? We do!"

Meanwhile, farther across the bridge, dozens of police officers began to assemble. They made a human line, three deep, while others behind them unfurled an orange net that stretched across the roadway's three lanes. When the protesters reached the line of police officers, many linked arms and prepared to stand their ground. A white-shirted police commander yelled via bullhorn that the marchers would be arrested for disorderly conduct. There was short pause as both sides held steady, then one officer reached into the crowd to pull a mask from one of the marcher's faces. The NYPD's chief, Joseph Esposito, grabbed the officer by the back of the belt and hauled him backward. But moments later, another officer plunged into the crowd and the standoff disintegrated into chaos.

For the next minute or so, police took the marchers who were at the front and restrained them with plastic wrist cuffs secured behind their backs. After the first dozen or so arrests, many of the marchers sat down or got on their knees, and tensions calmed once more. But the arrests continued. First by ones and twos, and then a half-dozen at a time, police arrested every protester who marched on the roadway. Some yelled their names to legal observers from the National Lawyers Guild, members of which would later file a class action in Manhattan federal court against Mayor Michael Bloomberg on behalf of protestors, accusing his police of leading marchers onto the Brooklyn Bridge and unlawfully using a trap-and-arrest technique to remove the protesters without cause.

Up the roadway, police seated the protesters against the sides of the road and began to take their information. More than 700 people were arrested, according to the NYPD; an officer who said he has worked large crowds many times said he would put that number closer to 1,000. It took almost three hours to flex-cuff the entire crowd and haul them all away.

Around 7 p.m., back at Zuccotti Park, the mood was a mixture of ebullience and concern. Legal observers worked their cell phones, trying to track down those arrested. Even with several hundred of their compatriots on their way to police precincts, more than a thousand people cheered on a drum circle, debated ideas and tried to dry off from the cold rain.

One woman at the Broadway entrance held a sign, quoting poet Gil Scott-Heron, that read, THE REVOLUTION

WILL NOT BE TELEVISED, which was a bit like saying the Gettysburg Address would be little noticed. Video of the seemingly indiscriminate Brooklyn Bridge arrests went as viral as the pepper-spray incident. Meanwhile, a theme began to coalesce. "The reason I'm here now is to speak for the other 99% of this country that has been denied a seat at the negotiating table," protester Henry James Ferry, who is a real estate agent, told TIME. "I don't hate capitalism; I don't hate rich people. I think you should come down to Wall Street and make as much money as you want. And when you do, you should pay a fair tax rate back to the city and the country that gave you the opportunity."

While the slogan "We Are the 99%" didn't originate with Ferry, his attitude encapsulated the frustration and anger of many of those who felt that the system had forsaken them. Protesters using the slogan began to appear in Los Angeles and Boston, as well as smaller cities like Chattanooga, Tenn., and Burlington, Vt. Soon, more powerful, organized forces were inspired to join the movement.

Joining Hands with Labor

On Oct. 5, many Occupy Wall Street protesters left Zuccotti Park in a march to Foley Square, a small park in the midst of Manhattan's most imposing collection of federal and state courthouses. They were joined there by several thousand members of more than a dozen labor unions. Police ringed the park with metal sawhorses, packing people shoulder to shoulder as they cheered to speeches by union leaders. Several hundred more people crowded the steps of the Manhattan Supreme Court, whose edifice was made famous by many episodes of *Law & Order*.

By now, the movement had a demographic following

far broader than that on Day One. On the march on Foley Square, a 5-year-old walked next to his mother, carrying a sign that read KINDERGARTNER AGAINST GREED. Murray Gittelman stood for hours in the square with his daughter and son-in-law, dressed in his sergeant's uniform from the 8th Air Force in World War II. His sign: WWII VET AND STILL OCCUPYING.

As the Foley Square march returned to Zuccotti Park, a group of protesters yelled, "Let's go to Wall Street!" and began trying to make their way down Broadway. Police had blocked off the entrances to Wall Street itself, and when protesters kept trying to enter the street, a confrontation broke out in which police reportedly resorted to using pepper spray again. A video of a police commander swinging his billy club in a crowd of marchers made the rounds online. Twenty-four protesters were arrested.

With Zuccotti Park's population stabilized at a few hundred, many protesters took up a routine of commuting to the park. On a warm afternoon in October, Jess Horner stood on a park wall in business garb. Horner, a licensed clinical social worker, earned a master's degree in her field from Columbia University but had been unemployed for the better part of a year. Every day, when she finished another round of job interviews, she came to the park and held a sign reading LICENSED SOCIAL WORK WITH NO JOB, NO HEALTH CARE AND THOUSANDS OF $ IN STUDENT DEBT. "This is part of my job search," Horner said. "I come here [and] meet and connect with people with similar ideals," including opposition to budget cuts in social programs that focus on the poorest and highest-risk people.

From the movement's beginning, I looked at the calendar as a harbinger of challenges to come. The Occupation began on a glorious early-fall day, but days and nights of cold rain reminded everyone that the harsh New York City winter loomed just around the corner. What kind of fortitude would the Occupiers show?

Occupy the World

Oct. 15 had been touted as a global "Day of Action," called for by the *indignados* protesting austerity measures in Spain. Beginning in New Zealand, the action moved west through Asia and Europe, where protesters railed against economic policies. In Rome, a giant, peaceful march erupted into riots after "a few thousand thugs," according to Rome mayor Gianni Alemanno, battled with police. In New York, the movement made its presence felt in the city's most famous spot. By 6 p.m., protesters had taken over much of the northern triangle of Times Square's famous X. Police set up barricades to keep crowds in the large open areas where revelers watch the New Year's Eve ball drop. About 5,000 protesters were split up into pockets, and when protesters on one side of an intersection yelled that they wanted to cross the street, and pushed against the barricades, police reinforcements arrived on horseback.

The mounted policemen nosed their horses into the crowd. Again and again they spurred them forward, using the animals' broad chests to bulldoze the barricades back into position. One of the police horses fell over, and its rider scrambled to get it back on its feet. Then, without warning, officers sprinted across the intersection, batons at the ready, pushing the barricades back against the crowd. "I saw them encroaching in," a cop said to his sergeant, pointing to a spot three feet from where I stood, where nothing had occurred. A scrum formed. In the center, a sweat-drenched police officer tried to pry protesters' arms apart. As the battle threatened to tip over into violence, a man wearing a white shirt with short sleeves and a bushy mustache calmly pushed into the middle of the melee. Chief Esposito, the highest-ranking uniformed member of the NYPD, pulled his officers back with one hand and pushed protesters away with the other.

Esposito had kept the standoff on the Brooklyn Bridge from spilling over into violence, and perhaps the protesters in Times Square remembered this. They started screaming, "Esposito! Esposito!" The chief gave a little wave. The protesters made an appeal to solidarity with the officers, chanting, "We do this for you." After 20 minutes, Esposito returned to the barricade, where protesters yelled that their only demand was to cross the intersection. Esposito asked if they would cross the street peacefully if the barricades were opened. After receiving an affirmative cheer, the chief nodded to one of his captains. The first wave of protesters streamed across the avenue. At each green traffic light, the cops opened more gates, and across they came, wave after wave. Pockets of protesters discussed their reasons for being there, and others told tourists what they had just witnessed. As quickly as the protesters had occupied Times Square, they relinquished it.

The answer to the largest of questions—What would the protesters do when winter set in?—came earlier than planned. Two days before Halloween, the crisp New York City autumn gave way to a brutal night of freezing rain and snow, coating the dozens of tents in Zuccotti Park. Organizers scrambled to tie down tarps over the group's media center. "People ask how we're going to get through the winter," a protester said. "We're going to dress warm, buy hot food from around here. We'll be fine."

The End of the Beginning

Finally, Mayor Michael Bloomberg decided the campout had gone on long enough. Shortly before 1 a.m. on Nov. 15, Occupy Wall Street's emergency-alert system blasted messages to allies and the media that the Zuccotti Park was being raided. The eviction had come at last. This time, without the benefit of advance warning, protesters couldn't assemble the thousands of supporters who had flooded in

---

The Rowdier Uprising out West

What happens to Occupy when violence enters the equation? The uprising's Bay Area branches, headlined by Occupation Oakland, produced early lessons about the fallout for both revolutionaries and authorities. From the beginning, Occupy Oakland has had a more aggressive vibe than its Wall Street counterpart, driven by a small core of activists who drew support from blue-collar workers and immigrants, punks and middle-class families. Public support surged in the aftermath of a police crackdown at the Oakland tent encampment on Oct. 25, when an Iraq war veteran was seriously injured, allegedly by projectiles fired by riot police. A few days later, Occupy Oakland led a general strike, drawing thousands who managed to shut down the country's fifth-largest container port.

Violence backfired for the activists too, however. On the day of Oakland's general strike, clashes broke out between police and masked agitators that saw more than 100 people arrested and dozens of businesses damaged. Blaming anarchists for the violence, Mike Porter, 24, a protester who had lived in the tent city since the outset, said, "They're totally taking advantage of our numbers and leeching off our

---

to defend the park a month before. With military precision, NYPD officers set a cordon and gave people minutes to leave or face arrest. Some grabbed what possessions they could and fled; about a hundred refused to leave and were arrested in short order. "Six hours later, the drone of police helicopters still reverberated around lower Manhattan," wrote TIME's Ishaan Tharoor, who was on the scene that morning. "But Occupy Wall Street's Zuccotti encampment, a site that inspired a global phenomenon, was gone."

---

movement. These people have no values." Kim Voss, head of the sociology department at the University of California, Berkeley, noted that radical elements of movements sometimes have a "net positive effect" at first, because they draw greater support to moderate groups and give authorities an incentive to offer concessions. "However," she added, "the opposite dynamics also occur, in which the radical elements erode support for movements and additionally justify repression."

In Oakland, the balance was tipped when a 25-year-old man was shot to death near the main encampment. While his involvement with Occupy was uncertain, his death helped embolden Oakland mayor Jean Quan, a veteran liberal activist who had come under fire for her handling of the protests, to order police to clear away the tents Nov. 14 because of "increased violence associated with the camp and the strain on our city's economy and resources." Said Edward, 24, a student standing in the rain with his sleeping bag: "I really believe in what's going on here; at the same time, I don't want to get beat up." The clearing went peacefully. Evidently, both sides had learned about the downside of mayhem.   —*By Jason Motlagh*

Coming just two days before Occupy's planned global Day of Action to mark the movement's two-month anniversary, the raid turned out to be the best p.r. an antiauthoritarian movement could hope for. On Nov. 17, hundreds of protesters marched on Wall Street, not succeeding in their goal to keep the New York Stock Exchange from opening but managing to display a fresh, angrier face of the movement. "Banks got bailed out! We got sold out!" the crowd chanted. Several police officers and marchers were injured in the scuffling, which escalated the drama of the day. Simultaneous rallies were staged around the city. Protesters told their stories in the subway. Hundreds of students assembled in Union Square protesting tuition hikes and high levels of student debt. Late in the afternoon, a crowd assembled to once again march across the Brooklyn Bridge, the site of mass arrests just a few weeks earlier when marchers took over the roadway. This time, 13 mounted police officers waited at the ready, but there was no need for action. Marchers stayed on the pedestrian walkway, where they found an almost eerie sense of calm. Protesters still called out chants, but without the buildings causing an echo, they drifted off over the cold water and into the night. Occupy Wall Street sent a message on its Twitter feed to remind protesters that it was a march, not a race, and to savor the experience. Finally able to cross the river, the marchers and the movement were entering a new phase.

2.
Hands Across the World

At a time when the U.S. often provokes resentment overseas, the Occupy movement inspired a very different reaction

BY ISHAAN THAROOR

As on many previous Fridays, Oct. 28, 2011, saw thousands of Egyptians rally in Cairo's Tahrir Square, peacefully voicing their anger at a military government many feared was undermining the country's hopes for democracy. On this typical Friday, Islamists formed the most vocal and organized throng in the crowds, demanding the resignation of the Egyptian army chief and the release of scores of detainees imprisoned by military tribunals. Half a year after the toppling of hated President Hosni Mubarak, the struggle for the future of Egypt raged on.

But there was another cause animating the protest: a cohort of demonstrators marched from Tahrir Square to the U.S. embassy. They weren't decrying American wars abroad, or Washington's support for the Egyptian military, but the brutality of the Oakland police after officers had assaulted Occupy Oakland demonstrators. One poster lofted in Cairo read, FROM TAHRIR TO OCCUPY OAKLAND AND THE USA, ONE GOAL: SOCIAL JUSTICE FOR ALL.

Yes, this display of solidarity was a mere sideshow to what's afoot in Egypt. But it's a sign of a unique moment in global political culture. For a populist American movement—the right-wing Tea Party ought to prove a study in contrast—Occupy Wall Street garners tremendous worldwide sympathy and support. And the respect goes both ways. While reshaping the conversation on political élites and corporate power in the U.S., many of Occupy's participants point to the inspiration and strength they draw from disparate struggles elsewhere.

That feeling of solidarity was on full display Oct. 15, when from Maine to Melbourne, hundreds of thousands of people marched in nearly 1,000 cities. The day of coordinated international action was instigated by Spanish activists to mark five months of their own protests over austerity measures and soaring unemployment. But it became, instead, the battle cry of the 99% and the moment Occupy Wall Street emerged on a world stage.

With the exception of the antics of a cadre of militant anarchists in Rome, the marches were largely peaceful; the cause of Occupy Wall Street was invoked in protests from Santiago to Tokyo. Thousands in London targeted the city's stock exchange. (Encampments in the heart of the capital remained weeks later.) Julian Assange, the controversial chief of WikiLeaks, spoke to the protesting crowd about the significance of the day: "What is happening here ... is a culmination of the dreams of many people all over the world who have worked towards them, from Cairo to London."

Assange was among a chorus of celebrities and intellectuals extolling the movement's virtues and railing against the excesses of a global plutocratic élite. Weeks into the occupation at Zuccotti Park, the Slovenian Marxist philosopher Slavoj Zizek, a leftist icon, delivered a speech to those gathered, placing the nascent American movement within a broader, long-standing struggle. "When you criticize capitalism, don't allow yourself to be blackmailed that you are against democracy," Zizek declaimed, his oft-rambling sentences echoed awkwardly back by the Occupy crowd's dutiful people's mike. "The marriage between democracy and capitalism is over." Zizek went on to invoke the success of China—supposedly the world's most dynamic capitalist society—as proof of his point, and as a mandate for the Occupy movement to start concretely thinking of a leftist, worldwide alternative.

From its very inception, Occupy Wall Street existed in an internationalist prism. Manhattan's Zuccotti Park was hailed an American Tahrir Square, a font for an American Autumn as that Cairo plaza was for the Arab Spring. The Occupiers, to many, were the American incarnation of Spain's antiausterity *indignados*, whose rallies had rocked Madrid and other Spanish cities for much of the summer. Days of action and protest were dubbed "days of rage," a gesture to recent, far bloodier episodes of dissent on the streets of Syria, Yemen, Bahrain and elsewhere in the Middle East. When some 700 activists were detained while marching across the Brooklyn Bridge, they were, according to some reports, "kettled"–corralled and arrested–in a manner similar to a tactic used by London's Metropolitan Police against student demonstrators frequently over this past year.

"We see ourselves as the continuation of this global movement," said Patrick Bruner, a designated press spokesman at Occupy Wall Street who spoke with TIME in October. "And it's now springing up in a place where most of the world's problems originated—Wall Street."

The most immediate inspiration for the group seems to have been the success of occupations and protests taking place across the Atlantic in Greece and Spain. Spanish *indignados*—the outraged—set up camp in Madrid and other cities across the country in May, enraged by the debt-ridden nation's turn toward austerity and the incapacity of hapless political leaders and global economic institutions to stave off catastrophe. The occupations of iconic squares like Madrid's Puerta del Sol provided the template followed now by American protesters in a growing number of cities across the U.S.

"Everywhere there is a great sense of confusion and disillusionment with traditional institutions of political and economic power," said Vicente Rubio, 32, a Spanish teacher in the New York City area originally from Zaragoza, Spain, and a regular at Zuccotti Park. "There's a general sense that all the struggles are connected." Rubio was more circumspect about what all these interconnected struggles may achieve: "It's important to consider this as a process, rather than something with definite goals and demands. We're trying to create a productive means to channel this feeling of discontent."

Those "productive means," first practiced in the squares of the Arab Spring, came to define both a summer of widespread antiausterity protest in Europe and the Occupy movement as well. A generation hooked on social media coalesced into supposedly "leaderless" movements, based on impromptu volunteerism and consensus-based forums like Occupy Wall Street's general assembly. Their encampments became festive spaces, pooling wide cross-sections of society. Drum circles and playful street theater were ubiquitous. "Of course, the focus is on the very real grievances we all have," said Bruner. "But at a basic level, this is really about making people happy again."

One of the largest and most striking protests took place in Tel Aviv, where an occupation protesting high housing prices in July eventually drew half a million people. "It's all part of the same thing. It's people saying, 'We want to be in charge,'" said Stav Shaffir, one of the early organizers there, speaking to TIME's Jerusalem bureau chief, Karl Vick. "As a movement that goes up against the most powerful force, if you act like an organization, like an institution, you lose. If you have one head, they know what to cut off. You have to be like water, to be everywhere, to be unpredictable. We work like an open code. Everybody should act their part. Everybody should act like a leader."

The Internet enables that sense of fluidity. "I think in a way what we see in the streets today is a result of things we were trained for, using the Internet since age 5," said Yonatan Levi, another organizer in Tel Aviv. "I think these assemblies are chat rooms, wide open, with this sense of nonhierarchy, that everyone is equal in the kingdom of the Internet, where there are no kings or queens. We've taken these tools that we've acquired unknowingly—this generation of ours, which was blamed for not doing anything in the world—and now we've taken these things we've learned out into the street. And it's pretty impressive, I must say."

But the tactics used during this year of global protest aren't simply the product of a newfangled technological age. David Graeber, an American professor at Goldsmiths in London and a self-declared anarchist, is considered to be one of the instrumental figures behind Occupy Wall Street. He claims to have been one of the first to plug the emblematic slogan "We Are the 99%" and, alongside a couple of Greek and Spanish anarchists, conducted training sessions with the clutch of activists who would eventually set up camp at Zuccotti Park.

Graeber, a veteran of the antiglobalization movement, specifically discussed how to establish and run the general assemblies that have convened twice a day in lower Manhattan ever since the Occupation began. It's a form of egalitarian "direct democracy" that he saw practiced not just in actions against the WTO by committed anarchists but also in an obscure corner of Madagascar where Graeber did research for his dissertation in 1989-91.

The community of Betafo—the subject of Graeber's 2007 book, *Lost People*—had effectively been abandoned by an enfeebled, impoverished state. With no recourse for outside help, residents began conducting their affairs autonomously and in a decentralized fashion, employing methods of consensus-based decision making now echoed in all the Occupation sites of the U.S. It's a sign of the movement's diverse origins that the habits of a marginalized community in a remote island nation could find their way into Occupy Wall Street's most fundamental institution. "When you experience something like this," said Graeber, referring to the general assembly, "it reminds you, things don't have to be the way they are. It changes your entire perspective about what can be achieved."

There are also more direct organizational influences on Occupy Wall Street. Activists in Tahrir Square have pointed to the Serbian youth movement Otpor! (Resistance!), which led a successful nonviolent struggle a decade ago that unseated the regime of President Slobodan Milosevic. Otpor! alumni had earlier visited Cairo and conducted training workshops with some of the embryonic, liberal dissident movements there—counseling civil society to adopt peaceful yet confrontational methods that, among other things, involve street theater, satire and the savvy use of media. Within a week of the Zuccotti Park occupation, noted Otpor! activist Ivan Marovic visited the site, likening this "first step" by Occupy Wall Street to that of astronaut Neil Armstrong on the moon.

Wherever that leap takes the movement (and mankind), it has clearly left a mark. Across the world, the slogans and rhetoric of the Occupy protests took flame. First popularized by the hacktivist group Anonymous, rebellious Guy Fawkes masks now appear in Occupation sites from California to New Zealand. In Hong Kong—an open port long the preserve of globe-trotting bankers—a tent camp started up in the heart of its financial district. Foreign governments took notice. The North Korean state news agency issued its own press release explaining the protests: "The waves of [demonstrations] which swept the U.S. recently is an expression of the grievances against the mounting social contradiction resulting from the worsening unemployment and the widening gap between the poor and the rich due to the serious economic crisis." That's likely one of the more reasonable statements ever produced by the pariah state's official mouthpiece.

In China, too, the official press initially greeted news of the protests with glee. Editorials in papers like the *China Daily* accused the U.S. media of deliberately underplaying the importance of the protest and belittling the Occupiers at the behest of the media's Wall Street paymasters and Washington clients. But as the protests endured—and mainstream U.S. coverage of the events improved—Beijing's smugness faded. China's version of Twitter started to censor any message invoking the word *occupy* in a bid to stymie local calls for protest. According to reports, police in Shanghai even started entering bars frequented by expatriates and interviewing Americans about whether they had anything to do with the Occupy movement taking place thousands of miles across the sea. After heavy-handedly stifling talk of the Arab Spring, Beijing's allergy to revolution kicked in once again.

That was predictable, considering the emergence of another high-profile ally of the Occupy Wall Street movement. Shen Tong, one of the firebrand student leaders at Tiananmen Square in exile, lives in New York City, not far from Zuccotti Park. He has been attending meetings with some of the more committed Occupy activists, offering what one participant described to the *Wall Street Journal* as "wise old man" counsel. "Last time we wanted a different China, we got shot at," Shen told the *Journal.* "America can still afford to do this nicely."

Still, the perennial question looms: What lasting change will such a tableau of protests actually achieve? There are no clear answers—nor international precedents—for this sort of amorphous uprising that has in its sights an entire constellation of political and financial élites. When he spoke to protesters in Zuccotti Park, Zizek, the Slovene philosopher, offered this stern advice: "The only thing I'm afraid of is that we will someday just go home, and then we will meet once a year, drinking beer, and nostalgically remembering 'What a nice time we had here.' Promise yourselves that this will not be the case." Zizek himself, though, soon departed.

The irony of a movement that has proliferated so widely and rapidly is that its central preoccupation remains survival in those local, small spaces where the flag of protest was first planted in the ground. Talk of grand political change is forever subsumed by daily updates on the risks of poor sanitation at Occupation sites and the threat of eviction. That, though, won't prevent countless people around the world from drawing the dots, connecting their causes with those of others worlds away.

Not long after the Tahrir protesters expressed solidarity with Occupy Oakland, a coalition of Cairo activists issued an appeal to the entire Occupy movement asking them also to fight against Egypt's backward slide toward military dictatorship. The statement read, "Our strength is in our shared struggle. If they stifle our resistance, the 1% will win—in Cairo, New York, London, Rome—everywhere. But while the revolution lives, our imagination knows no bounds." Even if this revolution ends up being simply one of the mind, many protesters will say it was worth it.

3.

The Leaders of a Leaderless Movement

By organizing into dozens of working groups,
Occupy puts the people in charge

BY STEPHEN GANDEL

In a society in which we're used to taking direction from Presidents and CEOs, captains and quarterbacks, Occupy Wall Street's leaderless structure seems like a formula for chaos. And yet this exercise in organized anarchy nonetheless gets a lot of things done. Crowds come together on cue. Messages go out to the media. Lawsuits are filed. Meals are served. Funds are raised (more than $500,000 by November 2011). And the silliest ideas, like building an igloo city in Central Park, get voted down. "There have been challenges, but generally the group has been effective," says Marina Sitrin, a sociologist who has written a book on leaderless movements and is an active member of Occupy Wall Street. "The lack of leadership has been able to get more people engaged in the process, which I think shows how effective it has been." So how does Occupy Wall Street make all this happen with no titles and no corner offices? By organizing as a network of dozens of working groups, Occupy Wall Street keeps its participants focused on particular tasks they can perform with autonomy and attention to detail. A look at the division of labor:

Idea Generation

The only power at first was the power of suggestion. Kalle Lasn, editor of the Canadian anticonsumerist magazine *Adbusters,* coined the name Occupy Wall Street and called for protesters to fill the streets of lower Manhattan. Catchy idea, but how to organize this? In August 2011, about 100 people showed up in lower Manhattan to talk about it, on the same day that Washington faced a government shutdown deadline because of gridlock over the federal budget deficit. Activists gave windy speeches calling for a list of demands, like a massive jobs program. According to *Bloomberg Businessweek*, David Graeber, an anarchist and influential activist, didn't like what he heard. He and a few others broke off from the group, formed a circle and started organizing the Sept. 17 march on Wall Street. Graeber proposed the slogan "We Are the 99%." By the end of the afternoon, nearly everyone had abandoned the original rally for Graeber's less formal discussion group, which became the model for Occupy's governing system. Meanwhile, untitled leader Lasn maintained the flow of ideas from up north. In early November, Lasn told a Canadian radio program that it would be a good idea for the Occupiers to leave the park before frustration and violence erupted. "Now that winter is approaching, I can see this first wild, messy, crazy Occupation phase kind of slowly winding down." He was right about the Occupation phase ending, but not slowly.

The People's Congress

Occupy Wall Street makes its decisions by consensus at what started as a nightly meeting called the general assembly, which draws a few hundred people, even when it rains. Facilitators run the meetings, but anyone is allowed to sign up to make proposals. Crowd members show approval by holding their hands up and wiggling their fingers. Downward wiggling fingers means you don't approve. Anyone can raise a finger to make a point. Rolling fingers means it's time to wrap it up. Since no bullhorns are allowed, the crowd repeats everything every speaker says, a technique dubbed the "people's mike." While the general assembly gets decisions made, a by-product is recruitment. At a time when many people believe government isn't working, the general assembly gives a sense of true democracy. A bit too much, in fact, as the group has grown larger and meetings about fund distribution have dragged on. "General assemblies need to go back to what they first were, which was a movement-building body," says Chris Longenecker, an original member. "They get people excited." By October 2011, the general assemblies had been pared back to every other night, and a smaller spokescouncil was created to make some of the group's decisions.

Getting the Word Out

The revolution has not only been televised; it has also been tweeted, tumblred and streamed. The Occupiers, mostly in their 20s, have been heavy users of social media to get their message to friends and the rest of the world. By November the group's Twitter account had more than 125,000 followers. Occupy Wall Street has two main websites: one that makes official statements, and another devoted to the group's meetings and day-to-day activities. The latter features a calendar of events and a list of Occupy's dozens of working groups, along with chat boards. According to that website in November, the media working group had 310 members and the Internet group 365. In a send-up of old media, Priscilla Grim, a former corporate social-media director, launched the *Occupy Wall Street Journal,* published as a newspaper by a volunteer staff of about 25, many of them working under assumed names to protect their day jobs. On the Tumblr microblogging service, the We Are the 99% site has thousands of pictures of people holding cards explaining whey they're part of that cohort.

Keeping It Legal (Mostly)

Even a group inspired by anarchists needs lawyers—a lot of them. By November, more than 1,200 protesters had been arrested in New York City alone. Early on, the National Lawyers Guild, a liberal advocacy organization, started a working group of lawyers to deal specifically with Occupy Wall Street. The guild has sent lawyers, identified by the special green hats they wear, to marches and rallies to witness arrests and take down names of those who go to jail. The guild runs a hot line that family members can call to get information. Guild lawyers have also represented many of the protesters in court, the vast majority of whom have decided to take their cases to trial rather than plea. Some of Occupy's most basic needs have produced legal battles, notably the necessity for portable toilets at Zuccotti Park. When police refused to allow them, lawyer Christopher Dunn of the New York Civil Liberties Union advised the group that it had to apply for a permit from the city agency that regulates street fairs. After much legal wrangling, the city finally agreed to a plan. Dunn acknowledges that representing a leaderless group has been a challenge. "It's not like you know for sure what they are going to do," said Dunn. "It makes it hard to negotiate with the other side."

Mobilizing the Marches

Occupy Wall Streeters may have no leaders, but from the beginning, the direct-action committee has had more sway over the group than others. In the argot of Occupy Wall Street, a march or protest is called a direct action. Unlike most other decisions that go to the general assembly, the direct-action committee has the power to pick and plan its event. Among the preparations the committee makes for marches is holding training sessions to teach members how to avoid violent confrontations with police and citizens. Longenecker, who has been on the direct-action committee since the protest began, admits that Occupy has made mistakes. In the first Brooklyn Bridge march, Longenecker says, he and others who planned the march wanted to give some of the protesters the ability to block the roadway and ultimately get arrested, if that was what they chose. A group of many hundreds went onto the roadway, many of them perhaps unsuspecting of their likely fate. At least 700, possibly more, were arrested that day, many more than planned. "We learned from it," says Longenecker. "But that march, our mistake, also put us on the map."

Creating a Culture

When planning a protest to denounce the growing economic divide between the richest Americans and the rest of us, you might not expect an arts and culture committee to be high on your list of priorities. But it was for Occupy Wall Street, which has roots in art. A group of artists called 16Beaver, named for the address of a downtown studio where they regularly meet, had long discussed occupying a public space as a form of performance art and were some of the first people to sign on to the movement. Since then, cultural creativity has seemed to spring naturally from Occupy Wall Street: regular poetry readings in Zuccotti Park, giant Halloween puppets of the Statue of liberty and Wall Street's *Charging Bull*. Most famous of all were the protest signs. In October, on the night before the mayor first threatened to remove protesters from the park, Jez Bold, Occupy Wall Street's unofficial curator, was busy packing up the signs to protect them. "Some of these are truly beautiful," said Bold. The People's Library, too, was an inspired creation. Situated in a corner of Zuccotti Park, it contained more than 5,000 donated volumes, including books from such leftist authors as Howard Zinn, Noam Chomsky and Naomi Klein, all organized according to ISBN. Said Zachary Loeb, one of a dozen librarians who volunteered to care for the books: "Information matters. We are feeding people's minds." The books were confiscated when police cleared the park, and many were lost, but like so much of what happened in the early days, the People's Library is now a permanent part of Occupy's colorful history.

The question is whether Occupy Wall Street, as it becomes more results-oriented, will start developing the kind of organization that it has so emphatically rejected so far. Already, the emergence of a high-level committee has caused grumbling in the ranks. Can the movement stay true to its grass roots and still change the country's direction? Sounds like a good topic for a general assembly.

MARY ALTAFFER/AP IMAGES

As part of a global "Day of Action" on the two-month anniversary of Occupy's launch, hundreds of protesters marched through Manhattan's financial district

SPENCER PLATT/GETTY IMAGES

Known as "Veterans of the 99%," current and former members of the military paused on a march in lower Manhattan

DON EMMERT/AFP/GETTY IMAGES

Before it was cleared out by police in a late-night raid, Zuccotti Park had become a tent city, fortified against the cold

SPENCER PLATT/GETTY IMAGES

An Occupy icon: a mask with the image of Guy Fawkes, who took part in a failed revolt against the King of England in 1605

MARIO TAMA/GETTY IMAGES

As the movement gathered steam in October, Occupy attracted labor-union support at a rally in Manhattan's Foley Square

YOSHIKAZU TSUNO/AFP/GETTY IMAGES

In Japan, a protester's mask says WE ARE THE 99% at an Occupy Tokyo rally during a worldwide day of demonstrations

CHIP SOMODEVILLA/GETTY IMAGES

In Washington, hundreds of protestors organized themselves into human numerals in solidarity with Occupy Wall Street

In a violent day of global protests, demonstrators in Rome set a government building afire and smashed bank windows

After earlier confrontations between Occupiers and authorities turned violent in Oakland, a protester makes a peace offering

SASHA BEZZUBOV (6)

Erin Cadet, actress–grad student

"It's a shame that there's an economic state that we feel like we have no recourse in our government, that we feel like we have to go out and protest in the streets."

Hari Simran Singh Khalsa, yoga teacher

"The exact concrete solutions may not have materialized yet, but the wonderful thing about it is, we're open to change and ready for some actual paradigm shift."

Katie Cristiano, organic farmer

"I don't think it's a Democratic or a libertarian movement. It's a group of people who are seeking to have their issues and their voices heard, regardless of their background."

Marcia Malkoff, social worker

*"I've marched many, many times:
antiwar, antinuclear, women's rights.
I was excited that young people were
getting involved again. I would like to
see it spread."*

Jess Horner, social worker

"This is the community-building that's necessary to make things happen when you do have demands—the prelude to something much larger and much more effective."

Robert Segal, wine salesman

"What brought me here? I used to work on Wall Street. I came down to validate their fears."

4.

Occupy, a Forum

*In interviews with TIME and elsewhere in
the public arena, prominent voices rose up to
define and debate the movement.
A sampler:*

THIS COUNTRY WAS BUILT BY MEN IN DENIM AND
WILL BE DESTROYED BY MEN IN SUITS.
—*Protester's sign at Occupy Wall Street*

❝ For the first time I can recall, the media and much of
the public are focusing attention on the nation's almost
unprecedented concentration of income, wealth and political power at the top. While the biggest question in
America these days is how to revive the economy, the
surge toward inequality is not unrelated. The vast middle
class no longer has the purchasing power to buy what the
economy is capable of producing. People could pretend
otherwise as long as they could treat their homes as ATMs,
but those days are now gone. The result is prolonged stag-

nation and high unemployment as far as the eye can see. The Occupiers are also bringing into sharp relief the consequences of all this for our democracy. The public's increasing cynicism about politics is due, in part, to the overwhelming role now played by money. That's to be expected when income and wealth have become so concentrated."
—**ROBERT REICH**, *UC Berkeley professor and former Secretary of Labor, to* TIME

❝ Since this movement started, I've been waking up in the morning without the dread (or at least without the total dread) with which I've woken every morning for so long, the vertiginous sense that we're all falling off a cliff and no one (or almost no one) is saying anything about it. In Zuccotti Park I felt a kind of lightening of a weight, a lessening of the awful isolation and powerlessness of knowing we're being lied to and robbed on a daily basis and that everyone knows it and keeps quiet and endures it—the terror of thinking that my own grandchildren will suffer for whatever has been paralyzing us until just now."
—**FRANCINE PROSE**, *writer and visiting professor at Bard College, on* occupywriters.com

❝ A lot of people seem very agitated about the fact that this movement doesn't have a list of sound bite–ready demands and media-ready spokespeople. Personally I'm delighted that Occupy Wall Street hasn't given in to the hectoring for a list of 'demands.' This is a young movement still in the process of determining just how powerful it is, and that power will determine what demands are possible. Small movements have to settle for small reforms; big ones have the freedom to dream."
—**NAOMI KLEIN**, *author and activist, in the New York* Times

❝ The young people in Zuccotti Park and more than 1,000 cities have started America on a path to renewal. The movement, still in its first days, will have to expand in several strategic ways. Activists are needed among shareholders, consumers and students to hold corporations and politicians to account. Shareholders, for example, should pressure companies to get out of politics. Consumers should take their money and purchasing power away from companies that confuse business and political power. The whole range of other actions—shareholder and consumer activism, policy formulation, and running of candidates—will not happen in the park."

—**ECONOMIST JEFFREY SACHS**, *director of the Earth Institute at Columbia University, writing in the New York* Times

❝ I understand the frustrations being expressed in those protests. In some ways, they're not that different from some of the protests that we saw coming from the Tea Party. Both on the left and the right, I think, people feel separated from their government. They feel that their institutions aren't looking out for them. The most important thing we can do right now is, those of us in leadership letting people know that we understand their struggles and we are on their side, and that we want to set up a system in which hard work, responsibility, doing what you're supposed to do, is rewarded."

—**PRESIDENT BARACK OBAMA**, *to ABC News*

❝ To everyone protesting right now. I want U to know I'm for peaceful protesting. Just try not to make the police feel like there the enemy. They will hurt U ... You would be surprised how many of them would like to be apart of protesting with U. There hurting to."

—**50 CENT**, *rapper, in three consecutive tweets*

❝ I believe that Barack Obama owns the Occupy Wall Street movement. It would not have happened but for his class warfare ... He sympathizes with it. And as it gets worse and worse, I believe this will be the millstone around Barack Obama's neck that will take his presidency down. As the American people look at Occupy Wall Street, what I believe that most of the American people say about Occupy Wall Street and all of its versions all over the country is, How about trying something different to help our economy instead of occupying Wall Street, and occupying Boston and occupying Oakland? How about you occupy a job? How about working?"

—**RUDOLPH GIULIANI,** *former New York City mayor, at the Defending the American Dream summit in Washington*

❝ Everyone has to follow the law, that has to be the starting place. But no one understands better [than the Occupiers] what the frustration is right now. The people on Wall Street broke this country. And they did it one lousy mortgage at a time. It happened more than three years ago, and there has still been no basic accountability, and there has been no real effort to fix it. "

—**ELIZABETH WARREN,** *Harvard professor, consumer advocate and Democratic candidate for the U.S. Senate, at a debate*

❝ We have a very capable financial-services sector that makes loans and allows business to start and thrive. Are there bad actors on Wall Street? Absolutely. All the streets are connected: Wall Street's connected to Main Street. And so finding a scapegoat, finding someone to blame, in my opinion isn't the right way to go."

—**MITT ROMNEY,** *Republican presidential candidate, at a town-hall meeting in New Hampshire*

❝ It's kind of like the Arab Spring, which was profoundly moving to me. Seeing all those young people interviewed in Egypt and Tunis. They knew what they were against, but they weren't sure exactly what they were for. They had a vision. They had no program, and they had no organized political party. That's the problem that the Occupy Wall Street people have."

—**FORMER PRESIDENT BILL CLINTON**, *interviewed by* TIME *managing editor Richard Stengel at Chicago Ideas Week*

❝ If you look at the data, one thing that's very clear is that the changes in the tax code, even between, let's say, the Clinton era and the Bush era, are very, very small compared to the huge changes in inequality we've seen. So very little of the changes we've seen are due to taxes. The inequality is almost all in before-tax incomes. So we can debate as to whether we want an extra few percent at the top or not, but that's not really going to do much to change the long-term trend ... I think one thing about opportunity in the United States: education is key. The more that we can provide students the opportunity to get on the first rung of the economic ladder by getting a good education, the better it would be for society overall."

—**ECONOMIST GREG MANKIW**, *former adviser to President George W. Bush, to NPR after his Harvard economics class was boycotted by students sympathetic to the Occupy movement*

❝ The Occupy Wall Street protest is atavistic. It's so unfocused. It is perfectly fine to join in protest, although I think this one is silly. People are trying to overturn capitalism? Come on. If people have the need to protest, they should protest for righteousness, to lift the yoke of oppression and to help those who are poverty stricken. They need to define

their mission. They are wandering around attacking free enterprise. However, somebody needs to tell them that socialism doesn't work. It hasn't worked in Europe and it certainly didn't work in Russia. It has never worked anyplace else where it's been tried. One thing about the Tea Party: they have definite goals. They want to cut government spending and the size of the government. These are defined objectives. [In contrast,] to occupy a park and just scream and tear things up is formless and without purpose."
—**PAT ROBERTSON**, *televangelist, to* TIME

❝ The budget office report tells us that essentially all of the upward redistribution of income away from the bottom 80% has gone to the highest-income 1% of Americans. That is, the protesters who portray themselves as representing the interests of the 99% have it basically right, and the pundits solemnly assuring them that it's really about education, not the gains of a small élite, have it completely wrong."
—**PAUL KRUGMAN**, *columnist and Nobel laureate in economics, in the New York* Times

❝ Where does Occupy Wall Street and its satellite movements go from here? The organizers need to become a major electoral block and make the case that they will get out the vote for leaders who support citizens' rights to First Amendment expression and will call for the defeat of city leaders who brutalize and suppress citizens ... Occupy has an ill-advised resistance in some quarters to engaging with the voter-registration process, but that may be changing. They are terribly vulnerable now without electoral organization and can expect only further violence and aggression. But if they register voters in recall drives and start to field their own candidates, they will send a powerful mes-

sage to cities' leaders that suppressing constitutional rights is a political death knell. The next place to Occupy? The voting booth."
—**NAOMI WOLF**, Give Me Liberty *author, on TIME.com; Wolf was arrested at Zuccotti Park on Oct. 18, 2011*

DUE TO RECENT BUDGET CUTS, THE LIGHT AT THE END OF THE TUNNEL HAS BEEN CUT OFF.
—*Protester's sign at Occupy Wall Street*

“ It was an inspired idea on the part of Montana Congressman Denny Rehberg to respond last week to the Occupy Wall Street movement with a call to Liberate Main Street. 'We're overtaxed in small business, overregulated, and over-litigated,' Rehberg said. More broadly, Liberate Main Street provides a rubric for a conservative agenda that contrasts with Occupy Wall Street. It would be an agenda that works to foster opportunity, not envy; that seeks change through democratic processes, not mob pressure; that encourages enterprise, not resentment; that enlarges the sphere of personal and civic freedom, not big government; that liberates Americans' energies, rather than pandering to their weaknesses; that acts to fix Wall Street's problems, not to demonize American business."
—**WILLIAM KRISTOL**, *editor of the* Weekly Standard

“ The media keeps asking this question: Who's organizing these Occupy Wall Street protests across the country? I am now going to reveal the names of the dangerous political radicals behind Occupy Wall Street. Ready? Here they are: Goldman Sachs. JPMorgan Chase. Citigroup. Morgan Stanley. Bank of America. Wells Fargo. And, their co-conspirators: most of Corporate America ... And, let me tell you, they are *really* good at political organizing. They have evicted millions from their homes. They have put millions of students into a virtual debtors' prison with outrageous student loans. They have guaranteed that 49 million shall live in poverty, and that 50 million go without health care. In doing these things they have awakened a sleeping giant. Who else could have gotten students and their grandparents, teachers and farmers, nurses and fire fighters, all working together? I couldn't."

—**MICHAEL MOORE**, *filmmaker and activist, to* TIME

❝ I think what you're seeing in America is questioning a system that has not served us very well. A system that ... is defined for corporate lobbyists instead of the best needs [of] the people. And people are feeling screwed a little bit there. And so the most important thing is not just getting swept up in the fervor of a fight ... If you're going to say one guy's bad, you've got to back it up with, 'This is how we fix it.' "

—**BRAD PITT**, *actor, speaking at a press conference to promote his movie* Moneyball

❝ It's impossible to translate the issue of the greed of Wall Street into one demand or two demands. We're talking about a democratic awakening. You're talking about raising political consciousness so it spills over all parts of the country. And then you begin to highlight what the more detailed demands would be, because in the end we're really talking about what Martin [Luther] King would call a revolution: a transfer of power from oligarchs to everyday people of all colors. And that is a step-by-step process. It's a democratic process. It's a nonviolent process. But it is a revolution, because these oligarchs have been transferring wealth from poor and working people at a very intense rate

in the last 30 years and getting away with it, and then still smiling in our faces and telling us it's our fault. That's a lie. And this beautiful group is a testimony to that being a lie."
—**CORNEL WEST,** *Harvard professor and activist, in an interview on the radio and TV show* Democracy Now!

❝ As a civil rights attorney, I worked with hungry children across Mississippi's Delta and invited Senator Robert Kennedy to visit the area in 1967. Kennedy was outraged by the depth of poverty and later urged me to tell Dr. Martin Luther King Jr. to bring the poor to Washington to dramatize their plight. We prepared to occupy the nation's capital in the summer of 1968 with people of every race excluded from America's prosperity. Even after Dr. King's death, people from across the country camped on the National Mall for more than a month, with nearly 7,000 in Resurrection City at its peak. Although many pronounced the Poor People's Campaign a failure, and while its promise was not immediately realized after losing King and Kennedy, it planted seeds that grew and made a difference. America needs a new transforming movement—not just for the poor but for the middle class and the entire 99%. I'm heartened to see dedicated citizens break the silence about glaring injustice and grotesque and growing inequalities that threaten our democracy. Occupy Wall Street, though inchoate and ragged, has helped shine a light in the darkness."
—**MARIAN WRIGHT EDELMAN,** *president of the Children's Defense Fund, to* TIME

❝ This revolution has no focus. But it does have a class system. On one end of Zuccotti Park sit the élite. They're young, overwhelmingly white, college-age kids banging

Mac laptops and yelling into iPhones before bedding down in Brooklyn. On the other end, mercifully separated by a mountain of tarpaulins, sleeping bags and human refuse I would not touch with a Hazmat suit, sleep the Smelly Ones. Standing downwind of this human biohazard isn't pretty. We're here at the protest epicenter, the planetary point where bitchery meets bellyaching. And it makes no kind of cosmic sense."

—**ANDREA PEYSER,** *columnist, in the New York* Post

❝ If protesters could contain their vitriol and temper their idealism with reason for even a moment, they might be more effective at articulating their own message and allowing others to be heard. Many Americans ... are just as angered as protesters are by government bailouts, college tuition hikes, dramatic job losses and spending power. Americans are livid about golden parachutes for corporate executives who walk away from disaster unscathed—and with enough money for five lifetimes. People are sick and tired of government undercutting programs that benefit the sick, the elderly and schoolchildren. The message of Occupy Oakland protesters resonates far and wide, but they must separate violence and vandalism from the cause."

—**CHIP JOHNSON,** *columnist, in the San Francisco* Chronicle

❝ I work three jobs. I have a house I can't sell. My family insurance costs are outrageous. But I don't blame Wall Street. Suck it up, you whiners. I am the 53% subsidizing you so you can hang out on Wall Street and complain ... If I could tweet advice to these protesters, it would be this: Get over yourselves, get off Wall Street, and get a real job."

—**ERICK ERICKSON,** *editor of RedState.com, on the* Huffington Post

❝ The Occupy protests could mark a significant moment in American history. I've never seen anything quite like the Occupy movement in scale and character, here and worldwide ... Since the country began, it has been a developing society, not always in very pretty ways, but with general progress toward industrialization and wealth. Now there's a sense of hopelessness, sometimes despair. This is quite new in our history. During the 1930s, working people could anticipate that the jobs would come back. Today, if you're a worker in manufacturing, with unemployment practically at Depression levels, you know that those jobs may be gone forever."

—**NOAM CHOMSKY,** *professor emeritus at MIT, speaking at Occupy Boston*

❝ We are called socialists, but here there is always socialism for the rich. They say we don't respect private property, but in the 2008 financial crashdown, more hard-earned private property was destroyed than if all of us here were to be destroying it night and day for weeks. They tell you we are dreamers. The true dreamers are those who think things can go on indefinitely the way they are. We are not dreamers. We are the awakening from a dream that is turning into a nightmare."

—**SLAVOJ ZIZEK,** *Slovenian philosopher-scholar, at Occupy Wall Street*

❝ It is not just the countries of the developed world that are witnessing increasing dissatisfaction. There is a thread that connects the anticorruption protests of India and Brazil, the Arab Spring protests against dictatorial regimes and the Occupy protests of the established capitalist world. The 'divine force' of market globalization has clearly benefited a few but has failed to positively affect the lives of many. The globalization of dissent has brought together an other-wise disunited and disparate majority against the centers of global finance. The Occupy protests are significant because they bring attention to the unaccountable power of global finance and markets, which are loyal only to their financial masters. Decision making must shift out of financial markets and into the arena of people and their democratic institutions. That is the writing on Wall Street."

—**ARUNA ROY**, *Indian social activist and a leader of the Right to Information movement, to* TIME

It moves my heart to see your awakened faces;
the look of "aha!"
shining, finally, in
so many
wide open eyes.

Yes, we are the 99%
all of us
refusing to forget
each other
no matter, in our hunger, what crumbs
are dropped by
the 1%.

The world we want is on the way; Arundhati
and now we
are
hearing her breathing.
That world we want is Us; united; already moving
into it.

—**ALICE WALKER**, *poet and novelist, on* occupywriters.com

5.
Are the Bankers to Blame?

Of course, but so are all the people who indulged themselves in creating the real problem: way too much debt

BY GEOFF COLVIN

It's a bit odd that the most popular Occupy Wall Street sign says, WE ARE THE 99%. The statement doesn't make accusations or demands. It just sits there, loaded with a narrative that the viewer has to unpack. Much is revealed by unpacking it, so if the protesters had more room on their signs, here's what they'd say:

"We've been through the worst recession in 70 years, and the economy is still terrible. Millions of us can't find jobs, and millions more are taking any low-wage, part-time, no-benefits job we can get just to make ends meet. All this was caused by a financial crisis that originated right here on Wall Street through the slimy machinations of you financiers, you who make more money than 99% of all Ameri-

---

Colvin is a senior editor-at-large for FORTUNE

cans. When your incompetently built financial system blew up, you got bailed out while we got fired and foreclosed on. A vast crime has been committed, and you got away with it. Now you're getting rich while we suffer."

The heart of the narrative, the source of the Occupy rage, is that last assertion: that Wall Street committed economic murder and not only got away with it but also was rewarded. Which leads to an obvious, critical question: Is it true?

In finding the answer, let's not be constrained by legal niceties, asking whether specific persons violated statutes. The central issue is whether Wall Street—the biggest investment banks, commercial banks and brokerages—deserves the Occupiers' rage for collectively causing the financial crisis and subsequent economic misery. To get started, we have to be clear on exactly what Wall Street did.

The big-picture answer is not complicated, even though some of the details are. Over the past two decades, Wall Street bought millions of mortgages from banks and other lenders around the U.S., then combined them, thousands at a time, into securities that investors could buy. To make the securities more attractive, the banks divided them into tranches (French for "slices"), representing levels of risk. The riskiest loans—those to borrowers who put the least money down or had the lowest incomes or credit scores— were in the lowest tranche, which thus paid the highest interest to investors. Each ascending tranche was less risky and so paid a lower interest rate. Investors could buy whatever mix of tranches they liked.

The basic idea wasn't new. Salomon Brothers had invented the business of securitizing mortgages in the 1980s. But this time around, several elements of the business were unprecedented. One was the nature of the mortgages; in the old days they were mostly plain-vanilla, fixed-rate loans to borrowers who had put down at least 20%, but now far more of them were exotic instruments with floating rates, interest-only options and other features that enticed borrowers who couldn't qualify for a traditional loan. More broadly, lending standards declined sharply; lenders were giving mortgages for more than the value of the property ("*We* pay *you* at closing!" said the ads) and giving them to borrowers without even checking their incomes. Subprime loans exploded from $35 billion in 1994 to $795 billion in 2005.

Why were banks willing to make such obviously dodgy loans? Because Wall Street was begging to buy them. How come? Because investors in the U.S. and around the world—not mom-and-pop but sophisticated institutions—were crazy in love with those mortgage-backed securities that paid returns 2 to 3 percentage points higher than more traditional securities, the risks be damned. In 1996, $493 billion of mortgage-related securities were issued; by 2003 the volume had mushroomed to $3.2 trillion. Mutual funds, pension funds and other investors sent word to Wall Street: Give us more of those mortgage bonds. Wall Street, in turn, said to America's mortgage lenders: Give us more mortgages to repackage. If you have to lower standards ... well, just do what you have to do.

When those mortgage-backed securities went bad, precipitating the disastrous financial meltdown, investors screamed: How could you sell us this junk? Wall Street responded, Look, before we sold you a bond we gave you a massive prospectus. It told you everything we're supposed to tell you. The decision to invest was yours—nobody forced you. Sorry it didn't work out.

While that response sounds evasive, plenty of evidence says it wasn't. The warning signs were visible well before the crisis, and some people recognized them. Hedge fund manager John Paulson saw what was coming and made $3.7 billion personally by betting the right way. Analyst Meredith Whitney and money manager Steve Eisman shouted from the rooftops that cataclysm was ahead; so did economist Nouriel Roubini. None of them had access to insider information. They just had those prospectuses and publicly available data, same as everybody else. If more people had studied as hard as the Cassandras did, there wouldn't have been much demand for Wall Street's mortgage-backed securities, so lenders wouldn't have pushed mortgages on every grownup with a pulse. The subprime debacle and subsequent crisis would have been a minor event, not a major one.

It takes two groups of willing parties to make a financial crisis. One group is lenders of money and sellers of securities—Wall Street—but the other is borrowers and buyers. If either group refuses to play, there's no crisis.

Not that they did it alone. Several other players were required in a crisis as big as this one. Rating agencies had given those mortgage-related securities high marks, in some cases triple-A, which is why the investors who bought them believed they didn't have to bother reading the fine print. The agencies later explained that the ratings are merely opinions that happened to be off the mark in this case; the agencies didn't mention that they're paid to rate securities by the companies that sell them.

Mortgage brokers, mostly small-time operators, got paid whenever they persuaded someone to borrow, regardless of whether the loan proved good or bad; some of them misled borrowers or plain lied, and many others just worked extremely hard originating mortgages. Washington policymakers, Republican and Democrat, created government incentives for mortgages to low-income borrowers, people who'd have a hard time making their payments if the economy tanked. Regulators failed to anticipate a once-a-century, system-wide blowout. Accounting rulemakers encouraged rampant lending by letting mortgage originators report profits as if they were getting all the income from a mortgage's entire life—up to 30 years—in the year the mortgage was written.

And then there were the borrowers: Americans of every station, from top executives to housekeepers. They bet that home prices would never stop rising or interest rates falling—knowing that if either trend turned on them, then their no-down-payment, interest-only, adjustable-rate mortgage could wipe them out. But they took the loans anyway. When the carousel stopped turning, they went to new websites like YouWalkAway.com, which explained how to abandon a home that had negative equity and stick the bank with the loss.

All those players combined to form a giant system that required each of them in order to function. Every player gained by being a part of the system, at least until 2007. None of them individually worried much about what the system as a whole was doing, which was just one thing: creating debt. Way too much debt.

That is the economy's fundamental problem now. Total U.S. mortgage debt increased from $3.8 trillion in 1990 to $6.8 trillion in 2000 to $14.6 trillion at its peak in 2008, a ballooning such as we'd never seen before. But we weren't just bingeing on real estate. Other consumer debt grew almost as fast, from $800 billion in 1990 to $2.6 trillion in 2008. Falling interest rates fueled the debt party by making loans easier to afford, and our main assets, homes and stocks, were appreciating, so we could add debt yet maintain our net worth. Many Americans were also in denial about their stagnating incomes; borrowing kept their living standard on the rise, at least for a while.

To spiraling personal debt add government debt, which has exploded since 2001. America's gross debt, meaning debt held everywhere in the economy, has risen from about 200% of GDP in 1990 to almost 400% today, as economist Kenneth Courtis points out. That "crushing debt load," he says, is "the core of the problem facing the U.S. economy."

It's the main reason the economy can scarcely grow and unemployment won't come down. We snap back quickly after old-fashioned inventory recessions (too much stuff and not enough buyers), but debt-based funks drag on. When virtually all the players in the economy are trying to reduce their debt at the same time, growth becomes almost impossible. And we've got ourselves deeper in the Valley of Debt than ever in our history.

With that perspective, it becomes clear what isn't the problem. Though the Occupiers complain about Washington's bailout of the banks, it didn't bring us to where we are. It averted financial Armageddon, and the banks repaid the government with interest. As taxpayers, the Occupiers made money on the deal.

Nor is our problem the appalling malfeasance of various lenders and mortgage brokers around the country. Yes, some of them pressured poor and elderly people into taking loans they didn't understand and couldn't hope to repay. Some blatantly misrepresented the terms of loans. Some banks broke laws by improperly foreclosing on borrowers, and some even repossessed the wrong homes. They should be prosecuted, and some have been. But those activities didn't cause the crisis and recession and 9% unemployment.

Our problem is too much debt. When the growing burden became unsustainable, when the market finally read the prospectuses and the economic data and realized that some of that debt wasn't worth much, we had a crisis and then a recession. We're still suffering because the problem hasn't even begun to go away. Consumers have reduced their debt slightly since the 2008 peak, but increased government borrowing has more than compensated. Gross debt is worse than ever. It's still unsustainable and has to be cut back, and that's the foundation of today's economic misery.

So, are the bankers to blame? Of course they are. This couldn't have happened without them. They were a major element in the giant system that produced so much debt. It's clearly just as true that the system wouldn't have worked without all the other players as well, so each of them is also to blame, at least to some extent. That raises the question of why the Occupiers are camped out in Wall Street's front yard rather than somewhere else.

But the answer is obvious. The Occupiers are enraged by the perception of injustice. Wall Street got bailed out; we got laid off. Wall Street is making billions; we're on unemployment benefits, which are running out. One could make a strong argument that the injustice isn't quite so stark. Wall Street got whacked harder than any other industry, with two of the industry's five major players (Bear Stearns and Lehman Brothers) out of business; just in New York City, tens of thousands of employees, from executives to secretaries, are jobless, the great majority of whom never went near a mortgage-backed security. The industry has made no more money over the past five years than it was making 15 years ago, and in 2007 and 2008 it suffered the greatest losses in its history.

Wall Street is now subject to the most massive new regulation to be imposed on it since the 1930s, the 2,300-page Dodd-Frank act. It mandates hundreds of new rules, many of which are still being written in late 2011. Industry lobbyists are pushing to soften those rules, further infuriating the Occupiers, but the end result will still constrain the industry in important new ways. One of the most significant new rules, the Volcker Rule prohibiting banks from trading on their own account, takes effect next year. It's 300 pages long.

It's worth noting too that the government bailed out plenty of the ordinary Americans who participated in the giant system, first through a federal mortgage-refinance program two years ago. Not many people signed up because it required evidence that borrowers could actually afford a mortgage, so a new program does away with all that. It offers new mortgages without proof of income at the lowest rates ever seen. If you were a responsible borrower and have more than 20% equity in your home, you don't qualify. The program bails out the most irresponsible borrowers, among others. Sounds familiar.

Of course that doesn't matter. Wall Streeters are the least sympathetic of any group in the giant system, and they don't deserve sympathy; the surviving bankers still make tons of money and know their business is more volatile than almost any other. And they helped the system work. They bear responsibility.

As we watch and hear the Occupiers' rage, let's just remember why our economy is suffering. We have too much debt. Everyone who contributed to that is to blame.

6.
The Citizen Who Stood Up to the Bankers

When one of America's biggest banks wanted to levy a new fee, a 22-year-old started a petition. Guess who won?

BY ELIZABETH DIAS

When Bank of America announced its plan to charge customers a $5 monthly debit-card fee in September 2011, it probably did not count on a young woman standing in its way. But for Molly Katchpole, a 2011 college graduate who was working two part-time jobs in Washington and living paycheck to paycheck, the annual increase of $60 was just plain unacceptable. "I heard the news about the fee, and was like, 'That is it. I'm sick of this,'" says the Rhode Island native, whose father is a machinist and mother a physical therapist. "On the one hand, the bankers are running a business, but on the other hand, it is people's money they are working with, and some people don't have a lot of money. It's not like they are just selling toothbrushes—it goes much deeper than that."

So Katchpole turned to Change.org, an online platform that posts petitions and mobilizes community campaigns. Immediately, her open letter to Bank of America to drop its plan for the new fee went viral. She closed her Bank of America account, cut up her debit card on camera and moved her money to a community bank. And Americans flooded her with support. One month and 306,000 signatures later, she won: Bank of America abandoned the proposed extra charge on Nov. 1.

Katchpole's success testifies to the power not just of protest in the Occupy era but also of social media's growing power to create solidarity. "Ten years ago if this had happened, what would Molly have done? Molly would have been mad, she would have been frustrated, and she would have quietly and meekly gone and moved her account to a community bank. That would have been it," says Change.org founder and CEO Ben Rattray. "With social media it's actually possible to connect other people and to build a lobbying group of customers for any business and any social institution."

Since the group started four years ago, Change.org has made possible more than 50,000 petitions in more than 30 countries. Some 500,000 new users join the site every month, 1,000 campaigns are added each week, and at least one petition achieves victory every day. But Katchpole's campaign has been the site's largest yet. Change.org's growth began to explode about one year ago, when organizers made a decision to shift emphasis away from giant catchall campaigns that lobbied President Barack Obama or Congress to manageable projects that solved local community problems. From baseball fans asking the San Francisco Giants to make an *It Gets Better* video to South African lesbians fighting the practice of "corrective rape," Change.

org petitions have become a new way to harness discontent worldwide—social, economic or political. "It is not enough just to be angry, and it's not enough just to tweet," says Rattray. "You have to coordinate people."

Across the U.S., financial and political frustration has spawned a rush of petitions to effect change at a time when Americans have lost confidence in Congress to get the job done. Katchpole's campaign wasn't the first to take on Bank of America, which came under the Change.org spotlight in the summer of 2011 when a Seattle woman won her fight to keep the bank from foreclosing on her home. Foreclosure petitions were one of two trends Change.org noticed on its site that year. Deportation cases against undocumented students was the other. Dozens of students have had their deportation canceled as friends and family used the platform to bring attention to their situation. After Katchpole's campaign, more than 30 copycat petitions have demanded that banks, including Citibank and SunTrust, change their fee plans. Nearly half have already won.

Many of the nation's largest banks, including Bank of America, JPMorgan Chase and Wells Fargo, initially considered new debit-card fees to make up for financial losses after Congress's Dodd-Frank act and Durbin Amendment limited the fees they could charge to retailers that accept the cards. But Katchpole feels that should not entitle them to simply pass along the fees to customers, which disproportionately affects low-income consumers vs. wealthy ones. "People kept trying to explain it along the way. I'm really tired of the lack of thought of people in charge of things," she explains, recalling how a Bank of America executive called her to explain the fee. "The reason these acts were passed was because of a lack of responsibility on part of the banks. So, no, I'm not going to go after Congress. I'm going to go after the banks because they are the ones that screwed this up in the first place."

Coinciding with Katchpole's campaign was another effort pressing big banks to put their customers' concerns first. Bank Transfer Day, a movement started on Facebook by Los Angeles art gallery owner Kristen Christian, 27, rallied customers to unite on Nov. 5 and switch from national banks to credit unions. It was a remarkable success. The Credit Union National Association reports that the day brought 40,000 new members to credit unions nationwide, adding some $80 million in new savings-account funds. As word about the event spread in the month leading up to it, nearly 650,000 new credit union members signed up, bringing $4.5 billion in new savings-account deposits. Whereas Katchpole and Christian have never met, Katchpole applauds her work: "If you have the luxury of being able to change banks, do it."

Even so, Katchpole argues that transferring accounts only partially solves the problem. "People have been saying that it is easy to switch banks, and it isn't," she says, recalling how she used to live in a Washington neighborhood where Bank of America was the only banking option. There are hassles of canceling one account and opening another, and many people's banking choices are influenced by gas prices, public transportation costs and work hours. "You can't ask some people to go out of their way, to take the Metro, to join a credit union," she says.

A sensitivity to the real-life constraints on most consumers is precisely what Katchpole—and the groundswell of the Occupy Wall Street protesters—feels that Big Business increasingly lacks. "Bank of America was thinking about its profits," says Katchpole, who has the word *empathy* tattooed over her right collarbone. "You might say, 'Well, that is what business is.' But I reject that. I think that business can be operated in way that takes people into account. And I think that needs to start happening more."

While Katchpole is not affiliated with the Occupy movement, her attitude resonates with many of the thousands who have taken to the streets to make their frustration known. But often their actions have tended toward general protest, without a specific course of action. After Bank of America announced its proposed fee in late September, Los Angeles Occupiers responded by blocking the bank's ATMs with yellow caution tape. Message delivered. But Katchpole and Christian showed that there may be many complementary ways to accomplish change, in their cases by tackling problems directly and using social media to create overwhelming popular demand.

Bank of America has yet to say how much Katchpole's petition influenced its decision to remove the $5 charge. Instead its refrain remains the same. "We received a great deal of feedback from customers, from community stakeholders and from interested parties. In light of that feedback, and in light of the competitive conditions in the marketplace, we decided not to proceed with the fee," company spokesman Ernesto Anguilla said. Other top national banks have dropped their plans for a debit-card fee. And if any of them decide to impose other questionable charges, they likely know now that such plans will face similar scrutiny.

As for Molly—whose hero, she says, is Hillary Clinton—her newfound public recognition gave her hope of a successful career beyond her freelancing in political communications and her work as a nanny. Several political and social-justice groups reached out to her with job opportunities, having noticed that she just helped push one of America's largest banks to change its policies. Says she: "It does really give me a sense of empowerment." And she's not alone.

7.

What Ever Happened to Upward Mobility?

*Why the U.S. has become the land of less opportunity—
and what we can do to revive the American Dream*

BY RANA FOROOHAR

America's story, our national mythology, is built on the idea
of being an opportunity society. From the tales of Horatio
Alger to the real lives of Henry Ford and Mark Zuckerberg,
we have defined our country as a place where everyone, if
he or she works hard enough, can get ahead. As Alexis de
Tocqueville argued more than 150 years ago, it's this dream
that enables Americans to tolerate much social inequality—
this coming from a French aristocrat—in exchange for what
we perceive as great dynamism and opportunity in our society. Modern surveys confirm what Tocqueville sensed back
then: Americans care much more about being able to move
up the socioeconomic ladder than where we stand on it. We
may be poor today, but as long as there's a chance that we
can be rich tomorrow, things are O.K.

But does America still work like that? The suspicion that the answer is no inspires not only the Occupy Wall Street (OWS) protests that have spread across the nation and beyond but also a movement as seemingly divergent as the Tea Party. While OWS may focus its anger on rapacious bankers, and the Tea Party on spendthrift politicians, both would probably agree that there's a cabal of entitled élites on Wall Street and in Washington who have somehow loaded the dice and made it impossible for average people to get ahead. The American Dream, like our economy, has become bifurcated.

Certainly the numbers support the idea that for most people, it's harder to get ahead than it's ever been in the postwar era. Inequality in the U.S., always high compared with that in other developed countries, is rising. The 1% decried by OWS takes home 21% of the country's income and accounts for 35% of its wealth. Wages, which have stagnated in real terms since the 1970s, have been falling for much of 2011, in part because of pervasively high unemployment. For the first time in 20 years, the percentage of the population employed in the U.S. is lower than in the U.K., Germany and the Netherlands. "We like to think of America as the workingest nation on earth. But that's no longer the case," says Ron Haskins, a co-director, along with Isabel Sawhill, of the Brookings Institution's Center on Children and Families.

Nor are we the world's greatest opportunity society. The Pew Charitable Trusts' Economic Mobility Project has found that if you were born in 1970 in the bottom one-fifth of the socioeconomic spectrum in the U.S., you had only about a 17% chance of making it into the upper two-fifths. That's not good by international standards. A spate of new reports from groups such as Brookings, Pew and the Organization for Economic Co-operation and Development show that it's easier to climb the socioeconomic ladder in many parts of Europe than it is in the U.S. It's hard to imagine a bigger hit to the American Dream than that: you'd have an easier time getting a leg up in many parts of sclerotic, debt-ridden, class-riven old Europe than you would in the U.S.A. "The simple truth," says Sawhill, "is that we have a belief system about ourselves that no longer aligns with the facts."

The obvious question is, What happened? The answers, like social mobility itself, are nuanced and complex. You can argue about what kind of mobility really matters. Many conservatives, for example, would be inclined to emphasize absolute mobility, which means the extent to which people are better off than their parents were at the same age. That's a measure that focuses mostly on how much economic growth has occurred, and by that measure, the U.S. does fine. Two-thirds of 40-year-old Americans live in households with larger incomes, adjusted for inflation, than their parents had at the same age (though the gains are smaller than they were in the previous generation).

But just as we don't feel grateful to have indoor plumbing or multichannel digital cable television, we don't necessarily feel grateful that we earn more than our parents did. That's because we don't peg ourselves to our parents; we peg ourselves to the Joneses. Behavioral economics tells us that our sense of well-being is tied not to the past but to how we are doing compared with our peers. Relative mobility matters. By that standard, we aren't doing very well at all. Having the right parents increases your chances of ending up middle to upper middle class by a factor of three or four. It's very different in many other countries, including Canada, Australia, the Nordic nations and, to a lesser extent, Germany and France. While 42% of American men with fathers in the bottom fifth of the earning curve remain there, only a quarter of Danes and Swedes and only 30% of Britons do.

Yet it's important to understand that when you compare Europe and America, you are comparing very different societies. High-growth Nordic nations with good social safety nets, which have the greatest leads in social mobility over the U.S., are small and homogeneous. On average, only about 7% of their populations are ethnic minorities (who are often poorer and thus less mobile than the overall population), compared with 28% in the U.S. Even bigger nations like Germany don't have to deal with populations as socially and economically diverse as America's.

Still, Europe does more to encourage equality. That's a key point because high inequality—meaning a large gap between the richest and poorest in society—has a strong correlation to lower mobility. As Sawhill puts it, "When the rungs on the ladder are further apart, it's harder to climb up them." Indeed, in order to understand why social mobility in the U.S. is falling, it's important to understand why inequality is rising, now reaching levels not seen since the Gilded Age.

There are many reasons for the huge and growing wealth divide in our country. The rise of the money culture and bank deregulation in the 1980s and '90s certainly contributed to it. As the financial sector grew in relation to the rest of the economy (it's now at historic highs of about 8%), a winner-take-all economy emerged. Wall Street was less about creating new businesses—entrepreneurship has stalled as finance has become a bigger industry—but it did help set a new pay band for top talent. In the 1970s, corporate chiefs earned about 40 times as much as their lowest-paid worker (close to the norm today in many parts of Europe). Now they earn more than 400 times as much.

The most recent blows to economic equality, of course, have been the real estate and credit crises, which caused housing prices to plummet and thus erased the largest chunk of middle-class wealth, while stocks, where the rich hold much of their money, have largely recovered. It is telling that in the state-by-state Opportunity Index released by Opportunity Nation, a coalition of private and public institutions dedicated to increasing social mobility, many of the lowest-scoring states—including Nevada, Arizona and Florida—were those hardest hit by the housing crash and are places where credit continues to be most constrained.

But the causes of inequality and any resulting decrease in social mobility are also very much about two megatrends that have been reshaping the global economy since the 1970s: the effects of technology and the rise of the emerging markets. Some 2 billion people have joined the global workforce since the 1970s. According to Goldman Sachs, the majority of them are middle class by global standards and can do many of the jobs that were once done by American workers, at lower labor costs. Goldman estimates that 70 million join that group every year.

While there's no clear formula for ascribing the rise in inequality (via wage compression) and subsequent loss of mobility to the rise of China and India, one key study stands out. Nobel laureate Michael Spence's examination of major U.S. multinationals for the Council on Foreign Relations found that since the 1980s, companies that operated in the tradable sector—meaning they made things or provided services that could be traded between nations—have created virtually no net new jobs. The study is especially illustrative of the hollowing out of the American manufacturing sector in that period as middle-wage jobs moved abroad. The only major job creation was in more geographically protected categories like retail and health care (another reason wages are shrinking, since many of the fastest-growing jobs in the U.S., like home health care aide and salesclerk, are low-paying).

That so many of the jobs we now create are low end underscores a growing debate over technology and its role in increasing or decreasing opportunity. Many of the jobs that have disappeared from the U.S. economy have done so not only because they were outsourced but also because they are now done by computers or robots. Advocates of technology-driven economic growth, like the McKinsey Global Institute, would argue that the creative destruction wrought by such innovations creates more and better jobs in the future; microchip making employs just 0.6% of the U.S. workforce, but chips make all sorts of businesses more efficient so they can develop new products and services. The problem is that those jobs tend to be skewed toward the very top (software engineer) or the bottom (salesclerk). The jobs in the middle have disappeared. According to the New America Foundation, a public-policy think tank, the share of middle-income jobs in the U.S. fell from 52% in 1980 to 42% in 2010.

While there's no doubt that so far, technology has been a net plus in terms of the number of jobs in our economy, a growing group of experts believe that link is being broken. Two economists at MIT, Erik Brynjolfsson and Andrew McAfee, have published an influential book titled *Race Against the Machine,* looking at how computers are increasingly able to perform tasks better than humans do, from driving (Google software took a self-driving Prius on a 1,000-mile trip) to sophisticated pattern recognition to writing creative essays and composing award-winning music. The result, they say, is that technology may soon be a net job destroyer.

The best hope in fighting the machines is to improve education, the factor that is more closely correlated with upward mobility than any other. Research has shown that as long as educational achievement keeps up with technological gains, more jobs are created. But in the late 1970s, that link was broken in the U.S. as educational gains slowed. That's likely an important reason that Europeans have passed the U.S. in various measures of mobility. They've been exposed to the same Malthusian forces of globalization, but they've been better at using public money as a buffer. By funding postsecondary education and keeping public primary and secondary schools as good as if not better than private ones, Europeans have made sure that the best and brightest can rise.

There are many other lessons to be learned from the most mobile nations. Funding universal health care without tying it to jobs can increase labor flexibility and reduce the chance that people will fall into poverty because of medical emergencies—a common occurrence in the U.S., where such medical crises are a big reason a third of the population cycles in and out of poverty every year. Focusing more on less-expensive preventive care (including family planning, since high teen birthrates correlate with lack of mobility) rather than on expensive procedures can increase the general health levels in a society, which is also correlated to mobility.

Europe's higher spending on social safety nets has certainly bolstered the middle and working classes. (Indeed, you could argue that some of America's great social programs, including Social Security and Medicaid, enabled us to become a middle-class nation.) Countries like Germany and Denmark that have invested in youth-employment programs and technical schools where young people can learn a high-paying trade have done well, which is not surprising given that in many studies, including the Opportunity Index, there's a high correlation between the number of teenagers who are not in school or not working and lowered mobility.

Of course, the debt crisis in Europe and the protests over austerity cuts in places like Athens and London make clear that the traditional European welfare systems are undergoing very profound changes that may reduce mobility throughout the Continent. But there is still opportunity in efficiency. Germans, for example, made a command decision after the financial downturn in 2008 not to let unemployment rise because it would ultimately be more expensive to put people back to work than to pay to keep them in their jobs. The government subsidized companies to keep workers (as many as 1.4 million in 2009) on the payroll, even part time. Once the economy began to pick up, companies were ready to capitalize on it quickly. Unemployment is now 6%—lower than before the recession—and growth has stayed relatively high.

The Nordic nations, too, have figured out clever ways to combine strong economic growth with a decent amount of security. As in Germany, labor and corporate relations are collaborative rather than contentious. Union reps often sit on company boards, which makes it easier to curb excessive executive pay and negotiate compromises over working hours. Worker retraining is a high priority. Danish adults spend a lot of time in on-the-job training. That's one reason they also enjoy high real wages and relatively low unemployment.

The final lesson that might be learned is in tax policy. The more-mobile European nations have fewer corporate loopholes, more redistribution to the poor and middle class via consumption taxes and far less complication. France's tax code, for example, is 12% as long as the U.S.'s. Tax levels are also higher, something that the enlightened rich in the U.S. are very publicly advocating.

No wonder. A large body of academic research shows that inequality and lack of social mobility hurt not just those at the bottom; they hurt everyone. Unequal societies have lower levels of trust, higher levels of anxiety and more illness. They have arguably less stable economies: International Monetary Fund research shows that countries like the U.S. and the U.K. are more prone to boom-and-bust cycles. And they are ultimately at risk for social instability.

That's the inflection point that we are at right now. The mythology of the American Dream has made it difficult to start a serious conversation about how to create more opportunity in our society, since many of us still believe that our mobility is the result of our elbow grease and nothing more. But there is a growing truth, seen in the numbers and in the protests that are spreading across our nation, that this isn't so. We can no longer blame the individual. We have to acknowledge that climbing the ladder often means getting some support and a boost.

8.

The New Generation Gap

What divides American most isn't race, gender, geography or ideology. It is the year we were born.

BY MICHAEL CROWLEY

Alexandra Serna cast the first presidential vote of her life in 2008, for Barack Obama, with enthusiasm and hope. Three years later, the 24-year-old, earning a degree in accounting at Florida Atlantic University (FAU), still supports the President. But her optimism has faded. "I think he's trying really hard," Serna says in a study room at the school's Boca Raton campus. Yet she's anxious about finding work after she gets her degree, and when asked whether she's politically engaged nowadays, she replies, "Personally, I'm not." While Serna isn't about to vote Republican in 2012, she hardly seems a sure bet to turn out for Obama.

Eating lunch in the food court of a sleepy shopping center 10 miles from the FAU campus, 78-year-old Walter Levy has few kind words for the President. The Navy veteran, who voted for John McCain in 2008, grouses about the state of the country and its government. "We're going backward right now," says the Fort Lauderdale resident. "The government's gotten itself too involved in everybody's life." His wife Concetta, 77, is more blunt. "I don't like the President's policies," she says. "I don't like Solyndra." The Levys are primed to vote Republican next year.

Listen to these three closely and you can hear the two Americas speaking. For the past several years, our political conversation has focused on great divides in our national life: red and blue, the coasts vs. the heartland, the 1% vs. the 99%. But the deepest split is the one that cuts across all these and turns not on income or geography but on age. In the past few national elections, young and old Americans have diverged more in their voting than at any other time since the end of the Vietnam War, according to the findings of an extensive Pew Research Center poll. The survey reveals that the youngest and oldest voters have strikingly different views on everything from the role of government to the impact of the Internet and suggests that the 2012 election could be one of the starkest intergenerational showdowns in American history, not just in Florida but coast to coast. Different generations rarely vote in lockstep; each is shaped by different formative influences. But this is something unusual. "We've got the largest generation gap in voting since 1972," says Andrew Kohut, president of the Pew Research Center. "Since 2004 we've seen younger people voting much more Democratic than average and older people much more Republican than average. And that may well play out again in 2012." Indeed, Pew's poll on generational politics shows a yawning generation gap in a hypothetical matchup between Obama and Republican Mitt Romney. Voters 30 or younger favor Obama 61% to 37%. Seniors over 65 choose Romney 54% to 41%. With Americans born from 1946 to 1980 (baby boomers and Gen Xers) almost evenly divided, the youngest and oldest voters stand in even starker contrast.

iPhones vs. IRAs

On one side are the millennial voters, meaning Americans born after 1980 who have come of age during the Clinton, Bush or Obama presidencies. Having lived through a period of dramatic social and demographic change, these voters harbor strongly liberal-leaning views about society and government. That's in part because the U.S.'s youngest voters represent change: about 40% of them are non-white. As a group they lean left on social issues—strongly supporting interracial and same-sex marriages by wide majorities. They believe government has a positive role to play even in seniors' lives. Millennial voters, like so many other Americans, consider themselves economically dissatisfied. And yet they believe, 46% to 27%, that life in the U.S. has improved since the 1960s, in part thanks to the technology revolution they have inherited. "I have an iPhone, and I would die without it," says FAU freshman Lizzie Barnes.

Whiter, less plugged in and feeling much grumpier is the Silent Generation, Americans over 65 who reached adulthood between World War II and the Vietnam War. The Silent Generation was profiled in a November 1951 TIME cover story that described its members as hardworking but docile and detached from political protest. Now in their 60s and 70s, members of this generation are restive, as likely to believe that the country has gone downhill as millennials are to think it has improved. They're more conservative than the so-called Greatest Generation seniors, who are older, remember the New Deal, may have served in World War II and are steadily passing away. "Part of what's going on is generational change," says Andrea Louise Campbell, an MIT professor who studies the senior vote. "Seniors who may have been socialized with memories of F.D.R. and the Depression are being replaced by younger cohorts of seniors for whom Eisenhower and Reagan are more relevant political figures."

Whatever the reason, today's seniors are nearly twice as likely as young voters to say life in the U.S. has changed for the worse, expressing that opinion 50% to 31%. They're particularly unhappy about social change, with only 22% saying a growing immigrant population has been a good thing and just 29% approving of interracial marriage. They're wary of the America that Steve Jobs built, dominated by new gadgets and technologies that many don't understand or use. Fewer than half of Silents—45%—believe the Internet has been a positive development. "You don't see the kids' faces anymore," says Sue Leese, 77, sitting outside a Bagel Works restaurant in Boca Raton. "They're constantly texting!"

Silent Generation members are twice as likely as millennials to call themselves "angry" with the government, and they trust Republicans more than Democrats on nearly every key issue. Obama appears to be a contributing factor in their discontent; they are the most disapproving of the job he's doing. How much of this disdain is a function of Obama's policies, and how much is a comment on his ethnic background, is anyone's guess. But some combination of the change he has championed and the change he actually represents is too much for some of these voters to accept. "There is this sense that comes out of the poll that Obama represents the changing face of America that some older people are uncomfortable with," says Kohut.

Many seniors resent any implication that race or ethnic background is driving their political preferences. "When I voice my opinion, I don't like being called a racist," Concetta Levy says. It is true, however, that white voters of all ages are more likely to strongly disapprove of the President. But strong disapproval of Obama and "unease" about him are dramatically higher among white voters over 65 than among millennial whites.

Apathy and Entitlements

And yet for both parties, there's a cautionary wobble in the simple notion of two generations colliding as the 2012 elections approach. The millennials and the Silents alike have deep qualms about their probable choices at the polls next year. That's especially true for the 30-and-under crowd. Although a massive turnout of voters like FAU student Serna helped carry Obama to the White House in 2008, young voters' approval of his job performance has plummeted. So has their interest in the political process. Four years ago, 28% of voters age 30 or younger said they had given a lot of thought to the presidential candidates. That number is down to a paltry 13%. Young voters also say they care less about who is elected President than they did four years ago, when the presidential race meant nearly as much to them as it did to their grandparents. Only 69% of millennials say they care "a good deal" about who wins the presidency, down from 81% four years ago. Such views suggest that many of those young 2008 Obama voters may be tuned out for good and that Democrats will do battle in 2012 without their most energetic foot soldiers. "They're not feeling loyal to the party," says Molly Andolina, a professor of political science at DePaul University who studies the youth vote. "Whether or not they're going to get out there and work in the trenches and show up on Election Day is a big question." Andolina

The New Generation Gap

also wonders whether the Occupy Wall Street movement could become a substitute outlet, beyond the political system, for the energy of frustrated young people. It's no wonder Obama has reached out to a younger audience of late through gestures like his new plan to relieve the crushing burden of student-loan debt and a series of Obama Student Summits.

Silent Generation voters, by contrast, appear, well, fired up and ready to go in 2012. They're more than three times as likely as young voters to be closely following the presidential candidates, and 84% say they care a good deal about who wins the next election. That makes them even more focused on this election than the millennials were in 2008. And they have already aced the dress rehearsal: young voters turned out in lower numbers in the 2010 elections, while the senior vote spiked in the midterms.

However, even as Silent Generation voters tilt heavily toward Republicans, they are hardly GOP loyalists. While they register a 39%-to-56% favorable-to-unfavorable opinion of Democrats, they dislike the Republican Party by a virtually identical ratio. The difference is that Silent Generation voters say they trust Republicans more to handle major issues like the economy, health care and immigration—with one exception: voters over 65 said they trusted Democrats to better handle Social Security. "That could undermine the Republican advantage" with seniors, says Kohut. That's all the more likely given that Silent voters care more about Social Security than any issue other than jobs.

Bracing for "Scare Tactics"

Which means you can count on hearing Obama and the Democrats talking nonstop in 2012 about how Republicans plan to slash entitlement programs, including Medicare and Social Security. Most Republicans counter that seniors don't have anything to worry about. Any such cuts, they say, like those in the budget blueprint of Wisconsin Congressman Paul Ryan, wouldn't touch benefits for voters currently 55 or older. "Republicans should expect the scare tactics that Democrats always go to," says Republican pollster Whit Ayres. Veteran consultants from both parties agree that a fierce Democratic message about entitlements helped the party win a longtime Republican seat in a May special election in New York State, where Democrats relentlessly attacked the GOP candidate, charging that she would rather slash Medicare and Social Security than raise taxes on the rich. Says MIT's Campbell: "Romney, I believe, is aware of this, and that's why I believe he's been careful to stick to a very moderate course on entitlement reform." Think of how the former Massachusetts governor pounced like a lion on his rival, Texas Governor Rick Perry, for calling Social Security a "Ponzi scheme."

For all the differences in their worldviews, the generations are not in direct conflict, the Pew poll found, a mildly heartening conclusion in a country divided in many other ways. They disagree, but they don't view each other as the enemy: millennials are about as concerned as Silents (57% and 59%, respectively) that there may not be enough money in the future to maintain Social Security and Medicare benefits at their current levels, which is a source of greater anxiety among the middle-aged Generation X and baby boomers (70% and 71%). Nearly every age group, including Silents, is concerned that sustaining those benefits might place too great a financial burden on younger generations, but the youngest Americans, who might have the most to fear from entitlement cuts, express slightly less concern than any other age group. If anything, the concern goes the other way: seniors seem ready to accept modifications in entitlements if it helps the next in line. In other words, young people don't want to pull the plug on Grandma to ease their student-loan repayments, while Silents don't reject the idea of means testing to spare their grandchildren a crushing debt burden. "I feel sorry for the young people," says Len Kaufman, 82, of Boca Raton. "We had a good run."

Things could still get tense. Although Washington has spent months deferring hard choices about the country's fiscal future, it may not be long before new austerity plans pit the generations in a clearer zero-sum game. For now, however, the young and old aren't competing. They are simply advocating two very different visions of what's good for, and about, the U.S. as a whole. And Obama's re-election may depend on which side speaks loudest in November 2012. —*With reporting by Hector Florin/Boca Raton*

Young vs. Old: A TIME poll shows how the generations view America differently

Seeing the 2012 Vote Differently

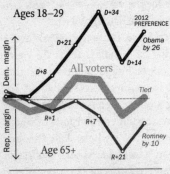

Ages 18–29

D+34
2012 PREFERENCE
Obama by 26

D+21
D+14

D+8

All voters

Tied

R+1   R+7

Age 65+
Romney by 10

R+21

Dem. margin
Rep. margin

2002 2004 2006 2008 2010 2012

Older Americans Are Less Enthusiastic About Growing Diversity

% saying each is a change for the better

- MILLENNIAL
- GEN X
- BOOMER
- SILENT

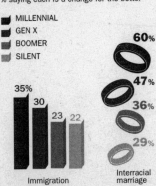

60%
47%
36%
29%

35%
30
23
22

Immigration

Interracial marriage

America the Exceptional, Or Not?

% saying the U.S. is "the greatest country in the world"

32%

Millennial
Current Age: 18–30

48%

Gen X
Current Age: 31–46

50%

Boomer
Current Age: 47–65

64%

Silent
Current Age: 66–83

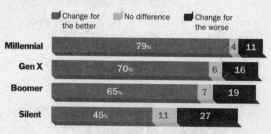

Silents Not Wild About the Web
% saying the invention of the Internet has been ...

Change for the better   No difference   Change for the worse

	Change for the better	No difference	Change for the worse
Millennial	79%	4	11
Gen X	70%	6	16
Boomer	65%	7	19
Silent	45%	11	27

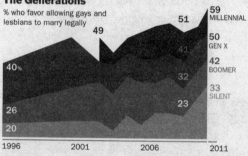

Same-Sex Marriage Divides The Generations
% who favor allowing gays and lesbians to marry legally

- 40%
- 49
- 51
- 59 MILLENNIAL
- 50 GEN X
- 42 BOOMER
- 41
- 32
- 33 SILENT
- 26
- 20
- 23

1996   2001   2006   2011

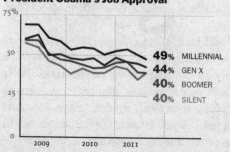

President Obama's Job Approval

75%

50

25

0

2009   2010   2011

- 49% MILLENNIAL
- 44% GEN X
- 40% BOOMER
- 40% SILENT

9.
Middle of the Road

*The people with megaphones get the most attention.
But the majority of Americans long for moderate politics.
A dispatch from our quiet, civil union*

BY JOE KLEIN

On a lovely Friday evening in September, in an affluent suburb of St. Louis, a group of neighbors got together to talk about their country. They were Republicans, Democrats and independents—the sort of people who keep up with the news of the day, always vote and often decide the winners of presidential elections. I asked them what was on their minds.

"Civility," said Jane Miller, a Democrat. "We can't seem to have a reasonable conversation about anything anymore, and it reaches right down here to our neighborhood. We're having this really ugly fight about deer. We're overrun with them. Some people want to kill the deer, others don't, and then there's a third group that wants to sterilize them. The argument has gotten really vile. People are acting crazy."

"Sterilizing deer is crazy," said Ed Hindert, a retired businessman. "You've got people out of work, the government running a deficit, and people want to spend money to sterilize ... deer?"

I nudged them toward the question of national incivility. "It all started with Newt Gingrich and the way he ran the Congress in the 1990s," said Bart Sullivan, an attorney who described himself as a moderate Democrat. "And now there's the Tea Party. The willful ignorance is incredible. They don't believe in global warming. They want to cut expenditures in the middle of a deep recession. How do you fight this anymore?"

I asked if there were any Tea Party supporters in the room. "I am," said Dan Amsden, the president of a systems-control firm. "The Tea Party is all about fiscal responsibility," he said and launched into a lecture about the vagaries of taxation, constitutionality, Nancy Pelosi, the Department of Education. It went on. Soon, Sullivan challenged him, and the two of them began wrangling back and forth, heatedly. The 20 or so people in the room watched this in silence, as if it were *Hannity* or *Hardball*.

All of which had taken 15 minutes. But Amsden had now assumed a certain dominance. He wasn't particularly loud or angry—he was quite intelligent, in fact—but he was persistent. He had views on everything. As we moved from topic to topic, Amsden always had a theory. There were others who spoke, but much of the group, especially the other Republicans in the room, lapsed into silence. Afterward, I took an informal survey of the silent Republicans, all of them men, and found that they didn't agree with Amsden's views. They were more traditional conservatives. I asked one why he didn't speak up, and he said, "I don't like to get involved in public disputes."

How to Build a Megaphone

The meeting in St. Louis—one of dozens of conversations I had during a 19-day road trip, south to north through the middle of the country—seemed a perfect metaphor for our national conversation: noisy activists, like the Tea Partyers and the anti–Wall Street protesters, were sucking the oxygen out of the room. And yet most of the meetings I attended, which were organized by TIME readers and CNN viewers, were not like that at all. They were populated by self-described traditional conservatives and moderate Democrats. Tea Partisans like Amsden were rare, although I did attend one Patriot Party meeting in Texarkana, Ark., in which Mitt Romney Republicanism was universally shunned. (Rick Perry, Ron Paul and Herman Cain were the candidates of choice.) Old-fashioned liberals were nowhere to be found; the Wall Street protest movement hadn't yet made the radar screen, although there was more anti–Wall Street bailout and anticorporate sentiment among the Texarkana Tea Partyers than among any Democrats I spoke with. Sullivan, the moderate Democrat who challenged Amsden, was typically cautious about government spending. "A lot of the stuff [Lyndon Johnson] tried in the Great Society ran amok," he said.

But the fascination with the Tea Party was universal; it was the dominant topic of conversation. Most people viewed the phenomenon with a mixture of horror and admiration. They opposed most Tea Party policies and were appalled by the bellicose rhetoric, but they were impressed by the fact that average Americans had built themselves a large enough megaphone to get the attention of Washington. Unlike the Wall Street protesters, the Tea Partisans have been clear about their agenda. Their congressional caucus staged the moral equivalent of a sit-down strike for smaller government—and escaped much of the blame for the resulting gridlock, which most people I spoke with placed at the feet of President Obama and congressional leaders. "The two parties can't come to a consensus even when the solution is obvious," said Jim Phillips, president of the Arkansas State Dental Association, who introduced me to some of his members over dinner at a country club in Jonesboro. He was talking about the federal deficit. The obvious solution, universally supported by everyone I spoke with except the Tea Partyers, was some variation of the $3 trillion deal that the President and House Speaker John Boehner nearly reached in July, with a mix of higher taxes and spending cuts.

"The Tea Party changed everything," said Billy Tarpley, who works for the dental association. "They said all the things people wanted to hear in last year's elections. A lot of it was coffee-shop talk"—the crazy, ill-informed stuff people growl about at the local café. As a result, he added, "nothing's getting done. I want to say to the Tea Party folks, You are now them!" There was a general sense that Tea Party mania was simmering down. "I used to think I was a libertarian," said Drew Ramey, who also works for the dentists. "I wanted government to get off our backs. But I guess I'm getting a little older. I like my roads now. I like my public services."

Sanity in the Heartland

Ramey's ability to stand back, look at himself and laugh was refreshingly common among the people I interviewed. When I made a road trip in 2010, the fear and anguish, the sense of American collapse were still raw. But then I traveled through the Rust Belt and talked to people whose home values had tanked, whose neighbors had lost their jobs. In 2011 I met more of the small-business people mythologized by the Republican Party, and I traveled through a more conservative part of the country. The people I encountered were a diverse group—I met with Latino activists in Laredo, on the Mexican border, and with a black women's book club in Austin—but there was a common, contemplative thread, as if Americans had been coming to terms with the scope of the economic disaster and trying to figure out what sort of expectations were reasonable for themselves, their children and the country. It seemed a quiet revival of the Great Silent Majority, grappling with drastic new circumstances. Their commentary was far more reasoned and thoughtful than the breathless tide of sensationalism and vitriol that passes for discourse on talk radio and the cable news networks.

Indeed, a TIME poll reflects the fierce sense of civility and moderation, and deep concern about the country's future, that I found all along the way. There is an overwhelming sense—81% of those surveyed—that America is on the wrong track, 71% believe the country is in decline, 60% believe the media and politicians don't reflect their view of what's really important, and a staggeringly wonderful 89% believe that politicians should compromise on major issues like the deficit rather than take a hard line. Nearly three-quarters think there should be higher taxes for millionaires. Only 11% identify themselves as supporters of the Tea Party; 25% say they're angry, but 70% describe themselves merely as upset or concerned about the country.

The Americans I spoke with were not rutted in ideology; they were open to new ideas. The black women in Austin had been watching the Republican presidential debates, and one of them, a lawyer, said she was interested in former

Senator Rick Santorum's notion of eliminating corporate income taxes on manufacturers. "That might get things moving again," she said, and none of the other women disputed her. The Arkansas dentists thought George W. Bush should have imposed a tax to pay for the wars in Iraq and Afghanistan.

There was tolerance for the President—outside of Planet Tea Party, where the most disgraceful and, dare I say, un-American insinuations still fester. Obama is assumed to be intelligent and honest. He is assumed to be trying hard to find compromises between the parties on most issues, and he is also assumed to be in over his head, a good man who has proved to be a disappointing leader. "He was always going to have some trouble down here in the South," said Mike Coats, a restaurateur in Conway, Ark., "because of existing prejudices."

"He might have had a shot if he hadn't come out so extreme," said Tab Townsell, the mayor of Conway, "if he didn't start out with health care and cap and trade, if he had stayed focused on the economy."

Townsell and Coats were part of a group of local business leaders assembled by a TIME reader named John Sanson, a young African-American Hewlett-Packard employee. We were having lunch at Coats' restaurant in downtown Conway, and it was striking, almost like time travel: these were mostly the sort of Main Street Republicans who had dominated that party in the B.T. era (before Tea). They had a story to tell about the revival of their city, largely accomplished with government subsidies. "We love earmarks," said Jamie Gates, a clever fellow who manages the local Chamber of Commerce and described himself as a Third Way supporter. Federal earmarks helped with the renovation of downtown, a pleasant tree-lined and flower-basketed area. Federal and state subsidies helped expand the local airport to accommodate corporate jets, while local funds built the infrastructure in an industrial park. The group even lobbied the Arkansas alcohol-control board to enable Coats to sell liquor by the drink in his restaurant. "We needed restaurants that could offer people a bottle of wine with their pasta," Gates said, "if we were going to lure new businesses to town."

And they succeeded: Hewlett-Packard agreed to set up a regional sales-and-service facility in town, with at least 1,000 new jobs. "There's been some pushback from the Tea Party folks about the price tag," said Townsell, "but most people in town support what we've done." The mayor added that he was worried that if the Tea Party tide in Washington continued to rise, cities like Conway wouldn't be able to grow and lure new businesses. "I've never voted for a Democrat for President in my life, but I might have to this time if it looks like the Republicans are going to control both the House and the Senate."

What's Wrong with America

In 2010, in the upper Midwest, talk of American decline was everywhere. There was a fair amount of anger directed at the Wall Street financial speculators who destroyed the housing market and at the Chinese for absconding with American manufacturing jobs. This year, in the lower Midwest, there was still plenty of talk about American decline—but it was surprisingly introspective. "The Chinese are screwed in the long term," said Gates of the Chamber of Commerce. "Their economy is artificially hyperproductive right now, but you can't fight Mother Nature." China's population is aging more rapidly than ours. "So there's an opening for us, if we put the pedal to the metal."

Most people were looking at the present, not the distant future, and they were far more pessimistic. "If I'm going to be really honest," said the Arkansas dentists' Jim Phillips, "in my gut, I think we've peaked." And who was to blame for American decline? There were two prevailing theories. The government was to blame, said the Tea Partisans and more traditional conservatives. There was a steady patter of protest against the growth of federal disability payments distributed by the Social Security Administration, which have taken the place of welfare for those without the physical or intellectual wherewithal to work—$48 billion a year going to nearly 8 million recipients, including more than 200,000 children suffering from attention-deficit disorder. "It's all about Big Pharma and their lobbying machine," said Sandra Powell, at the Patriot Party meeting in Texarkana. "They lobby to make ADD a disability so they can get a new generation of children strung out on Ritalin." (According to the TIME poll, 60% agreed with the Tea Party position on excessive dependency.)

There were similar feelings about government regulations, like the Dodd-Frank financial-reform act, which had made it more difficult for banks to give loans and small-business people to get them. "Most of our banks are solid," said Mike Beebe, the governor of Arkansas and a wildly popular Democratic politician, with an 82% approval rate. "But the feds did what they always do. They shotgunned that bill through, one size fits all. They should have concentrated on fixing the problems where they occurred instead of punishing people down here who were doing the right thing."

But there was a different, deeper conversation going on among those who didn't blame the government for all our ills—that is, among the vast majority of people I spoke with. There was a sense that the unprecedented affluence of the past 60 years had caused a certain lassitude, that we weren't working as hard as we used to. "Our parents had to deal with the ups and downs of life," said Renita Bankhead, a member of the Austin book club. "We've had so many ups that we never really learned how to deal with the downs."

One afternoon in St. Louis, I had coffee with five young men who were students at Washington University. Most of them came from privileged backgrounds, and they talked about how some of their classmates were shocked that there wouldn't be fabulous jobs awaiting them upon graduation. "I went to a private school in North Carolina," said Viraj Doshi, "and most of my classmates were lazy. They came from wealthy families, and they always assumed they'd have money and great jobs. All you had to do was go to college. Now they're lost." I asked whether that was true of women, who are graduating at a higher rate than men these days. The responses were rapid-fire: Oh, no, women work harder. There's a culture of slacking among the guys. Guys play video games more than women do. They watch sports on TV. "You go to the library," said Steve White, the TIME reader who had assembled the group, "and 75% of the people there are women."

There seemed a general agreement, across all the groups I met with, that Americans had gotten soft and lost their competitive edge. And there were very few remedies on offer. But Richard Meyer, a thoughtful orthodontist from Little Rock, Ark., raised one possibility over dinner with his fellow dentists: "Do we really need all this stuff we've accumulated? I can be a happy camper in a house half the size of the one I've got. I don't have to drive here in a BMW. Maybe we don't need to concentrate on consumer goods to be happy."

I remembered this great lyric by Bruce Springsteen,

"We'd better start savin' up/ For the things that money can't buy." The song stuck in my brain and reverberated when I got to Joplin, Mo., a few days later and spent a weekend there amid the devastation.

What's Right with America

"This is what a normal tornado looks like," said Mitch Randles, fire chief of Joplin. We were driving along the path of the tornado that destroyed a broad swath of the city on May 22. We were in a fairly affluent neighborhood on the southwest side of town. A few houses were destroyed, a few roofs torn off, trees downed. "It was like a Category 2 out here, which is what you normally get—some damage, some injuries, maybe a death." We drove east. In the next neighborhood, more affluent, there was a similar amount of damage even though the houses were brick and stronger; the storm was building strength, Category 3. We curled down a hill to a pond where one of the bodies had been found; a young man who had just graduated from high school had been thrown about a mile. And then up another hill and at the top ...

Category 5. It looked like Hiroshima. The devastation was almost a mile wide and 6 miles long. A few stray buildings still standing. It was just shocking. Bodies had been strewn everywhere, 162 of them; 4,000 homes were destroyed. Mark Rohr, the city manager, a big, quiet man with a severe flattop haircut, still teared up when he talked about what he saw that night. "We all have something in common now," he said. "We survived. And something has happened here. I call it the miracle of the human spirit."

Joplin, prestorm, was just another small city—a market and distribution center, a land of strip malls and chain stores: the Great American Anywhere. But it was different now. Jay St. Clair, one of 14 ministers at the College Heights Christian Church, talked about the ghostly, godly silence after the storm. Months later, the silence was still there in the tornado area; the only sound was the wind whipping through the stripped, bludgeoned and decapitated trees. The only possible reaction to the silence was awe, and the awe had informed a new sense of purpose.

Joplin's disaster was more cataclysmic for its residents than the 2008 financial collapse and deep recession that stunned the nation, but Joplin's reaction held some lessons for the rest of us. The Federal Government could help. There was gratitude that what could amount to $450 million in federal funds was on its way. But the crucial variable was not federal. A critical mass of Joplin's populace had been forced to become citizens again. They were activists now, intent on helping those who had suffered in the storm, and passionate about the shape and success of the city's recovery. They had taken charge of their future; they had regained the sense of community that so many other Americans had lost in the affluent wash of decades of good fortune.

That Sunday, the College Heights church, and some of the others in town and even some congregations from other states, held their eighth annual Great Day of Service. Thousands of people divided into work crews. The day before, thousands of young people had participated in a Cannabis Revival festival—America can be a brilliantly weird place at times—that had raised money for disaster-relief projects; the pot smokers and Evangelicals had found common cause in rebuilding their community.

I found a church group from West Virginia cleaning up a modest, middle-class neighborhood adjacent to the path of the tornado. They went door to door, asking residents if they needed any help, if they wanted their lawns mowed or raked. Pretty soon, the street was humming with electric mowers and trimmers, with rakes and brooms. I put away my notebook and picked up a broom. I worked with a big fellow named Todd. He told me about the various service projects he and his church had joined. There was always a feeling of accomplishment, he said. And he was right: the street looked a lot better after we had bagged the dirt and branches and refuse. I was going to ask Todd what he felt about the state of the country, but that suddenly seemed ... irrelevant. We were at work, on a beautiful Sunday morning, and it felt good. Todd was inspired by the Lord; I was inspired by Springsteen. We were both saving up for the things that money can't buy.

10.

Who Speaks for the 1%?

I do! They're just like the 99%, but they throw better weddings

BY JOEL STEIN

I don't like the top 1% of anything. Intelligence? Boring! Fun? Exhausting! Thoughtfulness? Annoying! Hairiness? Too hairy!

So I get why the Occupy Wall Street protesters gained momentum with their slogan "We Are the 99%." Everyone loves the 99%. You can have a beer with the 99%. You can eat with your hands in front of the 99%. You can talk about TV shows with the 99% without them telling you that while they don't think there's anything wrong with TV, if they had one, they would watch it literally all the time, so it's better to just not keep one in the house.

But I've met some of the top 1%, and on average, they're interesting, generous and charming. You know who is in the top 1%? Tom Hanks. You know who is in the bottom 99%? Not Tom Hanks.

It's not just that we admire the 1%. We need them. The 1% started Time Inc., creating my job. They founded Stanford, where I went to college. They funded Facebook and my mortgage. They created the Bill & Melinda Gates Foundation, bankrolled most great art, paid for medical research and created genius grants. No one has ever woken up early to gather around a TV to watch a wedding of two 99 percenters.

Part of the reason I'm defending the 1% is that while all the other journalists waste their time with the Occupy Wall Street losers, the 1% are available for some serious networking. But when I started talking to them, I learned that for all their supposed power, they are now too afraid to stand up for themselves. When I asked Kathy Griffin to explain why she and her fellow 1 percenters are a boon to society, she said, "I wouldn't touch that topic with a 10-foot pole made out of $100 bills I made from *Suddenly Susan* Season 2." Mark Cuban, the billionaire owner of the Dallas Mavericks who isn't even afraid of NBA refs, said, "I think there are financial engineers that add no value and fit the Occupy Wall Street stereotypes. They are the 1% of the 1% that f--k it up for everyone." In other words, Cuban is going with the rallying cry, "We are the 99.99%."

So I guess it's up to me to point out that all this anger about income inequality is misplaced because, unlike any other time in history, these days the 1% don't live that differently than the middle class does. Never before has $10 wine tasted so much like $1,000 bottles—and the $10 bottles come with pictures of cute animals! A $15,000 car breaks down as rarely as one that costs $250,000 and has far more cup holders. The middle class and the rich watch the same stuff on TV and in movie theaters, have equal access to Wikipedia and pay the same college graduates to do nothing but make us complicated coffee drinks. It is so difficult for the 1% to live differently that they have to collect art. Collecting art is so boring, there aren't any reality shows about it.

I get that we need someone to blame. People love the banker when they're borrowing and hate him when they have to pay him back. They also hate him when he claims to have mixed up the orange $500s with the light peach $100s and suddenly has a lot of cash even though he owns only Vermont and Oriental avenues. I don't know a lot about banking. But I do not believe that the worldwide recession was caused by financial derivatives created by the 1% who tricked the innocent 99%. I believe it was created by the great middle class who took out loans to live out the techno-bling dream we deified in rap songs and reality TV. Credit-card debt went up 75% from 1997 to 2007. We're now a nation of really poor people with a lot of frequent-flier miles.

The Tea Party and Occupy Wall Street are both right: We need government to get smaller and bigger. I'd argue for slashing middle-class entitlements but also adding services for migrant workers and that new poverty-stricken Muppet, Lily, who has to live on the same street as a monster who shoves cookies into his mouth just to let them fall right out.

But even I, who scored only in the 95th percentile on my math SAT, know that we are not going to dig out of our nation's debt just by jacking up taxes on the 1%. Raising that tax rate won't change the overall debt that much. We are all going to have to pay more and take less. Except for Lily. That poor girl can have whatever she wants.

Until people calm down and realize that, we should do something nice for the besieged 1 percenters. Invite Mark Zuckerberg to join you on FarmVille. Persuade your wife to e-mail Donald Trump a racy photo. Let Rupert Murdoch listen to your voice mail. Watch that godforsaken Oprah network. At least until they get through this hard time.

About the Authors:

GEOFF COLVIN is a FORTUNE senior editor-at-large, speaker, broadcaster and author of *Talent Is Overrated*.

MICHAEL CROWLEY covers domestic politics and foreign policy for TIME, where he is a senior correspondent in the Washington bureau.

ELIZABETH DIAS is a reporter in TIME's Washington bureau, where she covers religion and politics.

STEPHEN GANDEL is a senior writer for TIME and a blogger for TIME.com's The Curious Capitalist, for which he writes about the economy.

RANA FOROOHAR is an assistant managing editor of TIME in charge of economics and business.

JOE KLEIN is TIME's political columnist and the author of six books.

JASON MOTLAGH is a multimedia journalist who was, until recently, TIME's correspondent in Afghanistan. In 2010, he won a National Magazine Award for news reporting.

NATE RAWLINGS is a TIME writer-reporter and former Army captain who has written more than 20 stories on the Occupy Wall Street movement.

MICHAEL SCHERER is TIME's White House correspondent. He previously worked for Salon.com, *Mother Jones* and the *Daily Hampshire Gazette*.

JOEL STEIN is a columnist for TIME. His first book, *Man Made: A Stupid Quest for Masculinity*, comes out in May.

ISHAAN THAROOR is a writer-reporter at TIME and is editor of Global Spin, TIME.com's international affairs blog.